SANCTUARY

A Meditation on Home, Homelessness, and Belonging

Zenju Earthlyn Manuel

Wisdom

Wisdom Publications
199 Elm Street
Somerville, MA 02144 USA
wisdompubs.org

Library of Congress Cataloging-in-Publication Data
Names: Manuel, Zenju Earthlyn, author.
Title: Sanctuary: a meditation on home, homelessness, and belonging / Zenju Earthlyn Manuel.
Description: Somerville, MA: Wisdom Publications, 2018. |
Identifiers: LCCN 2017026926 (print) | LCCN 2018001195 (ebook) | ISBN 9781614293675 (ebook) | ISBN 1614293678 (ebook) | ISBN 9781614293491 (pbk.: alk. paper) | ISBN 161429349X (pbk.: alk. paper)
Subjects: LCSH: Home—Religious aspects. | Home—Religious aspects—Zen Buddhism.
Classification: LCC BL588 (ebook) | LCC BL588 .M36 2018 (print) | DDC 294.3/4—dc23
LC record available at https://lccn.loc.gov/2017026926

ISBN 978-1-61429-349-1   ebook ISBN 978-1-61429-367-5

22 21 20 19 18   5 4 3 2 1

Cover design by Tim Holtz. Interior design by Tim Holtz. Author photo by Vaschelle André. Set in Berkeley 11/15.

Wisdom Publications' books are printed on acid-free paper and meet the guidelines for permanence and durability of the Production Guidelines for Book Longevity of the Council on Library Resources.

♻ This book was produced with environmental mindfulness. For more information, please visit wisdompubs.org/wisdom-environment.

Printed in the United States of America.

Please visit fscus.org.

More Praise for
SANCTUARY

"Zenju Earthlyn Manuel's *Sanctuary* offers us much-needed clarity and light in a time of increasing violence and confusion, daily assaults on our basic sense of belonging."

— Gaylon Ferguson, author of *Natural Bravery*

"A lovely and timely contemplation—written with a poetic voice of interbeing, gracefully dissolving relative and ultimate truth into each other, compassionately embodying that place where political, spiritual, and cultural realities intersect."

— Ethan Nichtern, author of *The Road Home* and *One City*

"These remarkable essays by Rev. Zenju Earthlyn Manuel make us aware of the intimate relationship between home and sanctuary and the struggle between belonging and homelessness faced by many living under conditions of oppression, alienation, and dehumanization. A gifted story-teller, she offers an original look at how we might practice within the work of contemplative reflection, as well as a compelling portrayal of how that practice can be skillfully wed to a powerful and loving engagement with our world as it is. *Sanctuary* reminds us—at a critical moment of ecological anxiety, political unrest, and a renewed intensification of hate and misunderstanding—of the importance of embracing the deep abode of ancestry while simultaneously seeing the world afresh."

— Chaplain Doshin Nathan Woods, PhD,
University of the West

Contents

1

WHERE THE HEART LIVES

The Relationship Between Home and Sanctuary

———•◦•———

We are specks of dust on a strand of Mother Earth's hair. There is no need for us to "save" the Earth; we simply need to let her discard what has become stale. We need to release our planet of our wanting and begging, our ignorance and confusion, and be weaned from her breast, even when it feels we won't survive. When we stop exploiting the Earth, she will return to sustainability on her own and share her bounty generously.

In November 2016, America and the rest of the world were stunned when a candidate whose platform included harming immigrants and discriminating against certain citizens won the presidency. When I learned he'd been voted in, my heart sank, realizing that America had become even less of a place I can call *home*. Many of us had been living under a constant threat of harm for decades. Now, the blatant hatred ignored by so many others could no longer go unacknowledged. Many would recognize and join a shared sense of homelessness.

My parents were born and raised in southern Louisiana at the turn of the twentieth century, not far from the plantations where their ancestors labored as slaves, and where lynchings of their neighbors occurred often. While I'm certain they did not feel at home in that environment, there was sanctuary among others who embraced the black Creole culture. Because of *their* cultural sanctuary, I am able to experience a sense of home in my heart. Although I wasn't born or raised in the homeplace of my parents, grandparents, and great-grandparents, the bayou, swamps, music, foods, and eloquent Creole language were transmitted to me through my parents' very being. The cultural, ecological, and social life of Louisiana is in my bones, and whenever I'm there, I feel a primal sense of home—despite having never lived there.

Finding home, feeling home, and being at home are complex, multilayered, spiritual and cultural experiences independent of the place we live. Where is home? What is my true nature, and what does it mean to be at home with it? When I don't feel at home, where can I find sanctuary? These questions become critical when our lives are under threat.

In the early twenty-first century, groups are still being terrorized because of race, religious choice, physical ability, class, sexual orientation, and gender. Legendary radical feminist and academic Angela Davis points out that racism, Islamophobia, anti-Semitism, hetero-patriarchy, and xenophobia are, in fact, the ghosts of slavery. We have returned full circle to what catalyzed the civil rights movement and forced the creation of political and spiritual sanctuaries for those who were hunted by people trying to maintain white supremacy. In this book, I explore home and homelessness, sanctuary and refuge in the light of such terrorism and its impact on life, death, identity, and peace.

In spiritual communities, especially in Buddhist ones, the teachings on finding home are profound, but they often leave out the experiences of those who are dehumanized in their own homeland. Spiritual teachings like, "Home is within the heart" can be off-putting when loss and disconnection aren't also acknowledged. Those who have such experiences can feel homeless spiritually and physically, and finding refuge, or sanctuary, from acts of hatred must be offered along the path of finding our true home.

I was invited to give a talk at Deer Park Monastery in Escondido, California. When I arrived, I saw a sign in Thich Nhat Hanh's beautiful calligraphy that said, "I am home." When I saw it, the words rang through me as though I were hearing a temple bell. I felt relieved, and *my heart knew* I was home. I don't live at Deer Park, but reading the Zen master's words, I felt deeply at home. The home I felt isn't on the earth; it dwells in my heart. How was I able to recognize a home not visible but felt? Is a home like this momentary, or can I feel it wherever I go?

Deer Park, with its tree-covered hills, is a place where prayer, meditation, and song shape the sense of place and bring the visitor peace. It's a true sanctuary, offering immunity and refuge for troubled folks in troubled times. Sanctuary, from the old French *sanctuaire* and the Latin *sanctuarium* or *sanctus*, meaning "holy," is essential for those of us who live day in and day out in chaos and oppression, where belonging is never guaranteed. As I walked the monastery's paths, I affirmed in my heart that my true home must have peace.

What leads a person to homelessness? What happens when your home doesn't have the peace you'd hoped for? If we look at the impact of history, culture, and ancestry on finding home, we begin to understand the vastness of homelessness. The words "I am home" don't resonate for many who are marginalized by society. When we recognize the profound influence of social factors upon homelessness, then compassion, forgiveness, and similar virtues can carry us home.

If you have a sense of not belonging based on prolonged, systemic mistreatment, if you've been a target of hatred and violence, that disregard affects your well-being. In a relative sense, those who are dehumanized are never home. In the absolute sense, home is in the heart and cannot be touched by any outside force, even the most oppressive. Both senses are true. Oppressed groups live with the paradox that we are *and* are not home. While we are encouraged to make a home in this country, manifesting such is a struggle.

When I was eleven-years old, my family was having a tough time. One evening at dinner, the meat was stringy, and I asked, "Daddy, what's this?" My father proudly answered, "Possum. I caught it in the backyard." I didn't know what a possum looked like. All I could think of was the blood that might still be behind the house. I dropped the meat from my fork. My father, from the back roads of Opelousas, was doing what he'd always done to survive hard times. It wouldn't be long before we received our first—and last—bag of groceries from the welfare office. We were too proud to continue.

I remember saying to myself, *I will never be as poor as my parents*. I wanted to feel that I could get what I needed. And I know that when my father promised each of his three daughters a Cadillac and a house, he meant for us to be better off than he was. First, second, and third-generation African Americans who migrated north were supposed to succeed, and our progress was measured by external appearances. Most important was to have a roof over our heads. When you lose your house, you feel like a failure—a disappointment to yourself and your family.

Owning a home is a marker of stability and success, but today it's impossible for many of us to purchase property in the places we grew up. Imagine the assault on the heart when you are living in a homeless shelter or on the streets. How can we own the home we know and love? There are many ways to overcome physical homelessness. One is to redistribute wealth and return stolen territory. Another is to heal and disrupt the disconnections that result in disproportionate wealth, colonization, and occupation. When you consider the destruction of others' homelands and cultures and how it impacts their quest for home, the difficulty in overcoming spiritual homelessness is clear.

Enslaved Africans did not *immigrate* to America. In fact, many black people were here before the first colonists or slaves arrived. Native Americans did not give away their land; it was stolen. Holocausts for Jewish Americans, Armenians, Rwandans, and others did take place. Rape is used as a weapon against women. Muslims are harassed and annihilated. Perpetrators of all races murder transgendered people. What if those who have been pushed to the economic, political, and social margins were *seen* and their true histories revealed while presenting the teachings of finding one's true home? Would that help us understand the depth of our connections or disconnections to each other and facilitate the quest for an authentic home?

As I explore the epidemic of homelessness and the urgent need for sanctuary historically and in our time, I taste the tears of so many. How much longer will those who have been pushed out be able to survive? Is there too much water under the bridge to reconcile our disconnections from one another as people? If we are not paying attention to who and what is unacknowledged, we'll always have dangerous demagogues who shake us loose from the illusion that all is well. They are a curse and a blessing, as they help us remember what matters. Patience is more than waiting and hoping. Patience is taking the time to love what is difficult to love.

Sanctuary is the place we can go when our lives are under threat, where we can consider love in the midst of oppression. It's a place for those who speak a language not of the dominant culture, a place where anyone can say, "I am home."

Taking sanctuary is an act of saving one's life from the suffering of the world.

After one receives Buddhist monastic vows, homelessness and sanctuary become one and the same. This homelessness is an intentional disengagement from the chaos most people on earth endure daily. Monastics take refuge, and the spiritual life becomes their sanctuary.

I once met a nun of Buddha's forest tradition. I asked, "Where are you from?" She said, "Nowhere." I followed with, "I mean where do you live?" She said, "Nowhere."

My teacher was sitting nearby and overheard us. She said, "Ask where will she sleep tonight?" The nun lived nowhere but would be sleeping somewhere. The homeless mendicant smiled, and the conversation was over. Like Buddha, the earth was her pillow, the place upon which she would claim no territory, no country, no land, and no house. Instead she would trust the Earth as her mother to care for her. No matter where she lay her head, she wouldn't claim that place as her own. To some, this sounds romantic, to others too great a hardship to imagine.

At the other end of the spectrum, there are monks and nuns who have been exiled from their native lands, including the Dalai Lama and Thich Nhat Hanh. They were forced to leave families and sanghas and create new lives in foreign lands. To their credit, both have created potent sanctuaries for millions in duress and both became prolific in articulating the spiritual path. They did it as a direct response to the hatred and homelessness they themselves experienced. Sanctuary is a place you create when you are "missing" in the scheme of humanity. Establishing sanctuary is critical to finding home.

In this book, I explore a broad perspective on homelessness, physical and spiritual, and the act of creating sanctuary as a response to the hunger for home. I try to expand the spiritual teachings on finding home to recognize societal influences, the longing for connection to the earth and each other, and finding spiritual *and* cultural sanctuary. Along with this inquiry on sanctuary, I examine several kinds of home and homelessness including urban displacement; historical and political loss of land, culture, and language; as well as religious and spiritual quests for home. I dug my feet into the mud and waited to see what would emerge concerning the homeless condition of every living being—our insecurities, experiences, and threats to our sense of belonging.

Ultimately, this is a book about sustaining peace. I share from my heart the experiences I've had and the teachings that have settled in me. Please join me in entering the Dragon Gate, so we may each emerge with our own true face.

2

WHERE WE WERE BORN

The Soul and Home

———◆·◆———

I reviewed my secrets to be sure nothing hidden was revealed. What could be seen was only what I made of myself. No one knew who I really was or what I was capable of. Being afraid, breathing hard, the foul air held down for too long was forcing itself out. I pushed hard to birth myself, over and over, trying to get to the heart of the matter. Don't stop. She's coming. And she'd better be who she is or this time she will die. Here in this darkness, I return home from the far side of the moon.

To make the unfamiliar our own is a necessary act of survival. Many of us try to transform an alien home into one where we can flourish. The effort is as old as humankind.

People removed from their homelands brought their ancient observances into the rites of their new land, and as a result, world religions are suffused with indigenous rituals. Africans who were carried into this country as cargo reshaped the dominant beliefs into their own, and as a result, African deities and Christian saints intermingle. Christian hymns have African rhythms, and worship made to fit the African's sense of being home can be found in churches throughout the African Diaspora. The same is true of Native Americans and immigrants from Asia and elsewhere whose indigenous practices were forbidden yet found their way into Christian churches.

In a twenty-one day Zen Buddhist ceremony that begins in the home, I included three Haitian Vodoun deities that match in role to Zen's gatekeepers, protectors, and bodhisattvas. As I lit a candle at each altar, I called forth the Haitian spirits with their chants along with hymns to the Zen deities, and I touched a distinct and ancient place inside me. I could feel my blood ancestors, who had been forced from their homes and taken up Christianity, still having the need to invoke their own lineage and deities. I felt myself touching *home* saying Legba Atibon, Ayizan Velèkètè, and Erzulie Jan Petro, invoking at the same time Avalokiteshvara, and Bodhidharma. As I invoked the name of Shakyamuni Buddha as a great teacher, I invoked the sky by blowing an eagle whistle. Incorporating Vodoun deities into the Zen ceremony created a familiarity I found deeply resonant with home and therefore my heart.

At the same time, I felt afraid I'd be admonished for altering a Zen tradition that can appear set in stone. This, too, had an ancestral resonance, because Africans had to hide the things they added to their Christian rituals. As the fear subsided, it became clear that to shape religions to my own sense of home is to create sanctuary. Dogen Zenji took the practice of Ch'an he'd experienced in China and created Japanese Soto Zen. For all of us, our worship or our practice has to feel like home for us to embrace it.

Over the centuries, Buddha's path of awakening has been shaped according to people, places, languages, cultures, and times. Going from India to China, the teachings had to be shaped for the Chinese of the first century B.C.E. Then from China to Japan, from Korea to Vietnam, and from these places to the West, the teachings have been adapted each time. Once that is in place, we can authentically touch the wisdom of awakened ancestors.

We are born from our mothers. As we listen to our mother's voice, we come to know home as the place we'll be cared for. For some, caring might never arise or it can be disrupted. We may be placed with other relatives or care-takers, a foster home, or be adopted. The early loss of home brings a sense of not belonging.

Losing a home, individually or collectively, can also happen at any time, and we might spend the rest of our days trying to fill the void. Our grief can consume us.

Many years ago, at a Zen priest training, we sat in a cir-cle. The sun shone upon our faces. We were each asked by the group leader, "What was your deepest loss?" The leader was concerned we might seek what we feel we are missing from our future students.

When projection or transference becomes part of a teacher-student relationship, it needs to become conscious. When it was my turn to speak, my eyes filled with tears thinking about my deepest loss. I took a breath and said, "My deepest loss was my soul."

Trying to please my parents, my community, and the entire race of black people, I had separated from my true spirit. I spent so much time shaping myself into what was expected by others, to be accepted, to be seen as in the mainstream, I became a stranger to myself. I recognized the gap between my manufactured self and my soul, which I experienced as a kind of homelessness.

After the circle disbanded, a fellow priest said to me, "You might enjoy Case 35 of the *Gateless Gate*." It's a collection of Zen stories and verses offering perspectives on life, the self, and its relationship to the earth, compiled 800 years ago by Master Wu-men Hui-k'ai. Case 35 is about a woman separated from her soul.

Ch'ien-nu was the beautiful daughter of Chang-chien, who also had a handsome nephew, Wang-chou. In childhood, Ch'ien-nu and Wang-chou spent all their time together and cherished each other. One day Chang-chien said to his nephew, "One day I will marry you to my little daughter." Both children remembered these words. They went on with their lives, trusting that the two of them would live together for the rest of their lives. But when Ch'ien-nu grew up, her father accepted a request to marry his daughter from a man of rank (status). Arranged marriages were customary, and Ch'ien-nu and Wang-chou were grieved by this decision.

The next morning Wang-chou got a boat, bade farewell to everyone, and went up the river. In the middle of the night, he heard a voice, twice, and when he looked around, it was Ch'ien-nu. He was delighted. Ch'ien-nu joined Chou in the boat, and off they went to a nearby province to live together as they'd always dreamed. Eventually, Chou found a decent livelihood, they were married, and Ch'ien-nu gave birth to two girls. They lived happily for six years.

Then Ch'ien-nu began to grieve that she had abandoned her parents. She said to Chou, "We must go back and apologize for what we've done." Chou agreed and promised he would take her home.

When they arrived, Ch'ien-nu stayed near the boat while Chou walked up to the house, as it was customary for the husband to go to the house first. He looked back at Ch'ien-nu leaning against a tree and his two young daughters playing around her.

Chou, of course, was afraid Ch'ien-nu's parents would be angry, yet he walked up the path with courage. Surprisingly, when he got to the door he was received warmly, with open arms, by her father. Chou said, "I thought you would be angry with me for running away with Ch'ien-nu." The father was surprised. "My daughter has been sick in bed all these years, ever since you went away. Come. She's lying down." Chou followed his father-in-law, and when he entered the room, he laid his eyes on a thin and pale Ch'ien-nu.

He asked Ch'ien-nu's father to come with him, and standing near the boat he saw his daughter and two small granddaughters. He greeted Ch'ien-nu and invited her into the house. "Come, I have something to show you." As they walked toward the house, the sick Ch'ien-nu came out and met the well Ch'ien-nu. They recognized themselves in each other and came close enough to melt into one Ch'ien-nu. She said, "Now I don't know whether I'm the one who went away or the one who stayed home with Father."

Stories like these, shaped by the direct experiences of Zen practitioners, are meant to stimulate inquiry into our lives. Ch'ien-nu's two parts blending together was a homecoming. This koan speaks to the task of bringing together the fragments and images we hold, the parts of ourselves we abandon, and the journey home. Like Ch'ien-nu, many of us have become ill attempting to follow customs and beliefs that are counter to who we are and what we actually feel. You might find yourself masking or growing numb. There is a separation between soul or spirit and the strategized existence. I resonated with Ch'ien-nu not knowing who she was. I could understand that the two places—one healthy and one ill—expressed the separation she felt in her heart after her father's broken promise.

As a child, I experienced the broken promise of my Christian faith. My mother, father, and ministers told me about a love that included all beings. When I discovered there are people who hate others for the color of their skin, I became emotionally and spiritually drained and separated from my soul. I was both healthy and ill.

Thich Nhat Hanh is famous for saying, "Your true home is in the present moment." The home he speaks of is not only in time and space; it is in your heart. Is there peace, loving kindness, and warmth in your home? Is your home with you wherever you go?

One Saturday afternoon as a child I was watching cowboy movies on TV. Mom was in the kitchen cooking collard greens, candied yams, and a roast filled with garlic, the menu for guests from her homeplace of Louisiana. Gathering and feeding each other was the way we remembered where we came from. The adults got to speak Creole with all who'd found their way to Los Angeles. After they arrived in LA, they couldn't leave; they'd spent all their money getting there. The crowd ascended the staircase to the side door of our house, and at the top of the stairs, the men slapped Daddy on his back and the women kissed my mother and said, "Hey, Auntie." All the women were aunts; all the men were uncles, and all the kids were cousins, because we were all from the same place. We were members of the same tribe. This was how we acknowledged that we were home with each other.

Everyone told my mother how good the food smelled. You couldn't come into someone's house and ignore the smell of what was being created in the kitchen. And you couldn't come empty-handed. The women folk brought dessert or a special spice from Louisiana; the men brought beer and hunting rifles.

I'd be standing in the middle of this happy reunion when one of the adult cousins would come grab me and squeeze till it hurt. "Which one is this? The baby?" The real baby, three years younger, was so thin I feared they would break her, so I let them squeeze me, the middle child, for as long as they wanted. My older sister would be standing to the side waiting for the usual observation about how much she had grown. "And look at Sister," they'd say. "Sister" is what every eldest daughter is called in a Louisiana family.

After the greetings were complete, the women headed to the kitchen, the men to the den, and the smaller cousins sat in front of our black-and-white TV. I sat on the edge of it all, not knowing if I wanted to be in the kitchen and get fed like a puppy or hang with the cousins in the living room watching Mickey Mouse for the hundredth time. Out of boredom, I peeked into the den where the men were talking and laughing. They were all polishing their rifles, opening the barrels, and plunging straightened hangers in and out of them. Some spit and blew on the metal parts.

I sat up straight, checked around to see if anyone was watching. When the coast was clear, I slipped into the den with the men. The pink walls and purple vinyl sofa clashed with the gun-toting men, cigars, pipes, gold watches with wide bands, and Florsheim shoes. I smiled at each one, feeling especially cute among men. I smiled even more when they smiled back. They had all downed at least two beers. I looked back out the door. I had entered the forbidden zone and felt cute enough to stay a while.

Behind Daddy was a window that faced our busy street. The sounds of honking horns blended in with the hooting of men. Gold flashed from their mouths where their teeth had been capped, some just for style. I listened and laughed with them, although I didn't know for sure what they were laughing about. They were pullman porters, cooks, butlers, longshoremen, hustlers, gardeners, artists, dancers, singers, and chefs, descendants of people who lived off the land, who had bought homes for $5,000 and had gardens filled with yams, carrots, corn, and collard greens. And most of all, they were uncles and fathers. Their Creole bantering wasn't at all like the crying and whispering in the kitchen. I studied the six-story apartment building across the street, pretending not to listen to them talking about adventures in the backwoods, creating their own biographies.

The coffee table was cluttered with beer cans atop Mom's doilies. One man held his straw panama hat on his knee and a beer in his hand. He didn't have a rifle, and he looked lost without one, so I'm sure holding the can of beer helped. The room was filled with the drugstore cologne of countrymen who had just arrived in the big city. Smoke signals from their pipes made peace within and between them. I listened to the bus driving by the house as my shoulders began to slump, a sign of boredom. I leaned against Daddy, the second sign. Finally, I started squirming until he said, "Here take a swig of this." Without hesitation, I reached for his can of beer. All the men stopped talking. I enjoyed the silence; it meant I was the center of attention. I threw my head back and took a big swig. Then I wiped my mouth and gave that sound of a thirst being satisfied like I'd heard my father. The men howled.

Mom came running in. She saw me up on Daddy's lap. "Get down from there and come in the kitchen!" I can imagine the sight of a tiny little girl in a circle of men, guns, beer, and smoke. I had crossed into forbidden territory where men think, say, and do things different from women, and these things were not good for a little girl. I was not supposed to learn the ways of men.

On that Saturday afternoon, we ate together. The women stopped crying and whispering, the men put down their guns and softened into the warmth of the meal. My father ate, making smacking noises. I joined him making the same noises. We defied the unspoken demand to purge everything in us that was "country." If there were any worries, they weren't there that day. We were home. There was no contending with hatred, discrimination, or dehumanization for at least those eight hours. Until the sun went down, we were a village, a home, a sanctuary.

Lying in bed that night, I could see into the den. The purple vinyl sofa was folded out into a bed for Mom and Dad. Even though the men were gone, I could still see them gathered in the room with their polished rifles that now, in my mind's eye, looked like spears. Our den had been a refuge that day for the hunters, men who had ascended from the seasoned earth of the South. In a small place like our den, they belonged to each other in an ancient ritual of gathering. And I had been there with them.

We still had to contend with the hardships of leaving and losing homes, but that day home was where my heart was filled with love, the love of many generations. The feeling of that Saturday is still with me, an experience imprinted in my consciousness and my bones. Whenever it arises in the here and now, I am home.

Whether I'm walking down the street, sitting in a public place, or staying with a friend, when this warm, textured feeling emerges, I arrive back home, healing a trail of homelessness.

Home is knowing there is love, a God-given love that existed before time, arising from the same ancient place as homelessness. It is as primordial as the source of life. Home is inextricably tied to the original source of breath. When we can see the light through which we've come to Earth, we feel home.

Even amid cruelty and dehumanization, finding home is never more than a hair's breadth away.

3

WHERE THE SEA
DELIVERED US

The Need for Sanctuary

Ancestors, I'm at home, as close to the earth where your bones have settled. I climbed the clouds and saw your faces alight from resting. You remain in the very place the sea delivered you. I walk in your honor; your stories are now unburied, your spirits alive. I go forth speaking your names, feeling so close to your presence that anyone can see from the way I walk that you are inside me. If anyone yells as I cross the street wearing African attire, "This is not Africa!" I can respond calmly, "It certainly isn't."

In one sense, at the core of sanctuary is the failed quest to find home in the places we live. For centuries, millions have sought refuge from genocide, violence, economic loss, and political oppression, forced to venture into unfamiliar places. Some have climbed mountains, some have swum the seven seas, others have crossed deserts to save their families and their communities' lives. Millions have been forced to leave when their ancestral lands were destroyed; others have fled refugee camps that had become too dangerous to remain in, leaving generations of descendants with an insatiable yearning to return home. Displacement is an embodied experience, imprinted on our bones. Since the advent of nations and boundaries, the discarded have left home and their descendants have sought to find it again.

Spiritual teachers espouse that home is in the heart. When I ask, "Where do I belong?" they respond, "Look within." But it is difficult to find oneself without acknowledging the social and cultural dimensions of homelessness.

I look at indigenous peoples and tribes of all nations (African, Native American, and many more) who have been disrespected and disregarded on the homelands their ancestors lived upon as sacred for millennia, and my heart weeps for their lives and identities. Their children are homeless. What can we say to them? Be at home within their hearts? Without residing with dignity on the lands of their ancestors, this may feel impossible.

If the spiritual quest *to find home within* were enough, what do you do when your soul cannot live in peace on the land that is your birthright? Perhaps you've moved to an urban space where gentrification and the purchase of entire neighborhoods are displacing generations of those you know and love. Maybe your family home or farm had to be sold because of an unpayable mortgage or taxes or insurance.

My family had to move four times before I turned twelve. The first time—I was two years old—we moved to a two-story house and lived above a preschool my parents owned and operated. By the time I was seven, my parents rented out the upstairs room, and we moved to a plush house in a middle-class neighborhood, one of four black families there. Our house had five bedrooms, a maid's room, a courtyard with a pond and a fountain, a cottage behind the house, and a four-car garage. Relatives from Louisiana and Texas visited constantly, wanting to be in our house with the living room that was like a grand ballroom. Our success—the big house *and* a brand new Buick—meant attending a white, mostly Jewish school nearby. I was in third grade. My older sister was allowed to complete junior high at the all-black school in our old neighborhood, while my younger sister and I attended an elementary school in which we were two of the only three blacks.

The move was a culture shock. With my dark skin and fading Creole accent, I was different from the other kids, and the differences were unacceptable to the others. At eight years old, I didn't know how to survive the humiliation I experienced while barely able to keep up with the higher level of education at my new school. I didn't have a clue about timetables or multiplication. The other children were reading books as thick as the ones I had seen adults read. I kept quiet and when possible I disappeared into my desk. I longed to return to my old school and our old house, where my mother still worked in her preschool downstairs.

I stayed at the new school and made one best friend who was white and Jewish. We did everything together at school. We helped ring the recess bells, line up the students for vaccinations, and made flyers for the parents. But after school, I was not allowed to play with her.

Her maid told my mother that her parents were prejudiced. I didn't understand what that meant until sixth grade, when my friend and I signed up to take violin lessons at school. After months the decisions were made about who would be offered these special classes. As the names were being read, both of us perked up, confident of our acceptance because of our great service to the school. They read my friend's name and we celebrated by giggling into our hands. But my name was never read. I couldn't believe there wasn't enough room for one more child and that there wasn't one more violin.

My best friend and I left school that day barely speaking to each other. When I got home, I asked my mother why I wasn't chosen, and I watched her eyes drop. That night, I cried in my bed until it finally became clear to me. I wasn't white. I had moved from the black school where my identity was closely tied to our culture. My innocence vanished, and I learned that for some, love is conditioned. Once a talkative child, I grew quiet in the struggle to regain my balance. I felt a keen sense of loss, living in a world that favored white people.

My friend and I remained close until graduation. Under my influence we both signed up to attend the all-black junior high school my oldest sister had attended. Our parents were shocked for different reasons. In the end, she went to a private Jewish school and my family moved again.

As the property values and taxes increased in our Jewish neighborhood, the fees from my parents' pre-school remained modest. So, we sold our big house, paid our back taxes, and purchased yet another home. A huge moving van came and took us to Inglewood, which at the time was a white Protestant suburb just outside L.A., where homes were reasonably priced. The city of Inglewood is primarily populated by black and brown today, but in the early 1960s, there was only one other black family on our block. In terms of blatant racism, my life at school and in our neighborhood worsened, and the connection between displacement and dehumanization sealed together in my mind. Surviving meant assimilation. Not fitting in meant never feeling welcome, body and spirit never being at home.

These experiences of displacement followed me into adulthood and produced a perpetual fear of homelessness because of how I was embodied. In what neighborhood would I be welcome as a nonconformist, queer, black, woman? Where do I belong?

Similar experiences of homelessness occurred much later in my life. In 2013, my partner and I had fallen into serial homelessness, spurred by the quadrupling of rents in Oakland, California. We rented a home in Oakland and rented out a home we owned in Albuquerque. We tried to buy the home in which we were living in Oakland, so we sold our New Mexico home to have the funds. The bidding system for purchasing the home was not in our favor, and we didn't get the house. It led to six sublet agreements in other places, one after another, to stay in Oakland, and our savings dwindled.

As a Zen priest, I was asked by several people, "What lesson did you learn from losing your home and having your financial resources drained?"

I couldn't respond.

A quick answer would have minimized the emotions that were erupting inside me. I didn't want to reduce a journey into the depths of my suffering into a simplistic response. If I had been looking only for a physical home, it would have been easier. But I needed a place that would fill the ancient hunger for home that resides in me from an ancestral past.

My feeling of displacement has its roots in the African diaspora and the systemic dehumanization of blacks in the Americas and around the world. I needed time to reflect, to explore the nature of intergenerational homelessness without *figuring* anything out. I could barely breathe.

During my time of reflection, I met with the former owner of the home my partner and I had been unable to purchase. It was a beautiful day in Berkeley's Elmwood district. My former landlord and I each expressed our disappointment in our not being able to purchase her home. I tried to stave off feelings of victimhood, but the struggle persisted. As I continued, it became clear the sense of not belonging, the loss of language and culture, and the wish for a perfect home is imprinted on my bones. I saw that trying to purchase her home was an effort to resolve an experience of uprootedness that goes at least as far back as the slave trade. With this insight, I walked out of our meeting as if I'd never seen Berkeley before. I was in an altered state, feeling as lost as my ancestors must have felt when they landed in this country. My world had changed, and I was trying to reorient myself to a very new perspective. The loss of her home had uncovered what had been buried beneath each response to rejection my whole life. It marked the beginning of a slow, gradual path toward compassion.

Pema Chödrön, a nun and renowned western Buddhist teacher, reminds us that the mantra at the end of the Heart Sutra is meant to ease fear and cultivate compassion within suffering: "Gone, Gone, Gone Beyond, Gone Completely Beyond—Awake, So Be It." Yet we aren't transcending or going beyond suffering. Our lives are gradual paths of groundlessness. When we can accept that people and things are always shifting and changing, our hearts can open.

When we're overwhelmed by pain and suffering, or by groundlessness, we move to the next beyond. Pema Chödrön says we are developing a compassionate and patient relationship with our fear. The quaking in our lives is the very nature of going beyond, flexing and extending our heart muscle that is often stiff with arrogance, opinions, anger, self-righteousness, and prejudice.

The experience of renting six sublets, one after another during our period of homelessness, forced me to ask once again, "What is home?" Each time we found a physical home and experienced suffering, we were living out the mantra, "Gone, Gone, Gone Beyond, Awake." The experience wore down our fixed views of home and of life. As it became too much, we had to go back to basics, to the ordinary things of our lives, not waiting for a gigantic breakthrough but allowing the disintegration one step at a time. When fear, angst, frustration, or "why me?" arises, ground yourself in the ordinariness of your life and live one day at a time. Suffering teaches us this. When we suffer this much, we can only be still and take each moment as it comes.

Homelessness is like walking in a dark forest, step by step. It's an initiation. Feel into the mystery, not knowing what you might touch. In this way, homelessness can be the beginning of a new life even when it feels like the end. In the midst of an initiation, how you see life is tested and if you are open, it will transform you. Going forward, you'll see the world in a different way, as when I walked out of the tea-house in Berkeley and saw a new and different city. A gradual breakthrough of consciousness began when our bid to purchase the house was declined. The seed for transformation was planted.

Homelessness is more than just the loss of a physical home. It is also the loss of culture, connection, identity, and affiliation. This hunger for home is deep and wide, touching the nerve of ancient displacement and dispossession. In modern times, we see homelessness as a crisis of industrialization. But its roots are ancient and visceral, a trauma that passes from generation to generation.

Thich Nhat Hanh writes:

> Please call me by my true names,
> so I can hear all my cries and laughter at once,
> so I can see that my joy and pain are one.
>
> Please call me by my true names,
> so I can wake up
> and the door of my heart
> can be left open,
> the door of compassion.

I first heard this poem before entering the path of Buddha and recognized in it the cry for a lost ancestral home. The tears welling from deep inside me expressed a longing for connection with my origins, to know the ancient ceremonies, medicines, rituals, dances, and ways of the land that were lost in becoming American slaves. Later I realized that Thich Nhat Hanh is encouraging us to see ourselves *in* the other, to open our hearts to every living being, including perceived enemies, and to forgive everyone.

I couldn't do it right away.

I couldn't feel the interbeing of joy and pain. I couldn't digest the lines in his poem, "I am the twelve-year-old girl, refugee on a small boat, who throws herself into the ocean after being raped by a sea pirate. And I am the pirate..." I couldn't be both the mayfly on the river and the bird that eats me. I couldn't be the slave and the master, the one who hates and the one who loves, the oppressor and the oppressed.

I did not feel interrelated to other living beings as the poem teaches.

I had mountains to climb before I could reach that understanding.

A reflection on the naming of enslaved Africans helped to see more what was tangled with the feelings of homelessness. While other ethnic groups' names were changed at Ellis Island, enslaved Africans—more than *ten million* purchased and traded—weren't even considered human and were given the last names of their *owners*. While many have changed their names, most people of African descent still have surnames that are more like brandings.

My last name, Manuel, is Portuguese. King Manuel of Portugal, the largest slave trader of the time, brought Africans to the Caribbean, in particular Haiti, and so I carry his name, a man who was blind to my ancestors' humanity. Our slave owners' names are not without connection, because they evoke a relationship with our new origins in America.

Those who have reclaimed African names, been given them at birth, or when entering the priesthood of an African tradition, such as Ifá, Candomblé, Santeria, or Vodoun, still may work hard to fit in on the continent from which enslaved Africans were dispersed. It's not just that descendants of enslaved Africans have suffered enormously; we've had to do so without our names or knowing our blood lineages. For us, the effort to find our place can feel abstract, even numbing. Without our true names, it is difficult to consider anywhere home. The destruction of names, tribes, lands, cultures, languages, and truths, and the absence of documented lineages are a large part of our struggle. Wise spiritual teachers rarely consider this when they offer guidance for "finding home."

When the journey of finding home takes ancestral homelessness into account, we begin to understand the need for sanctuary in a new way. The hunger for home is deeply layered. When seeking a vision of being healed, multigenerational displacement motivates within some of us a desire for our indigenous lands of origin or to create sanctuary or shared community with those of similar ancestral origin, places where we can enter life fully without fear. We need places to breathe and heal our disconnection from the earth. Our spiritual journey requires us, first of all, to understand the pain of the loss of our ancestral identity and to experience the extent to which we have wandered. This loss of homes is in our bones and begs to be acknowledged, not merely transcended.

Those who have tasted dispossession through slavery, holocaust, war, ethnic cleansing, massacre, or forced migration are admonished by patriots, "If you're not happy here, go home!"

"I *am* home," we think, or even say, but we might not feel home in a place where we are told in many ways we don't belong.

A friend who lives in Haiti told me that in the Haitian *Kreyól* language, the word for home is *lakay*, which literally means "being at home."

This is significant because *having a home* and *being at home* can be entirely different experiences. Having a home conjures up a physical locale. We are born in a place, indigenous to some land, somewhere. We have residency, or citizenship. Among some Haitian people, it is important to know exactly where you are from. When first meeting, they try to situate you in relation to others. The question, "Where are you from?" literally means, "Where are you a person?" And if we are not *at* home, when homelessness is deep-seated and outside our control, where are you a person?

From the moment we acknowledge that there is discord between our homeplace and *who we are*, we no longer feel at home. Suddenly, we're uncomfortable with our surroundings and become distressed. We may find ourselves living on the streets, because we don't feel at home anywhere. Being at home is an experience in which our heart and spirit resonate with *the place* we dwell. It's being settled and still—as we are in sitting meditation.

Home cannot be an experience of shame, terror, or rejection, but one of safety, freedom, and being respected by others, experiencing love and being embraced, being known and knowing who you are.

During a difficult financial time, I lost my apartment on Lakeshore in Oakland. It was in the year 2000, when the rents of Oakland were increasing dramatically, and I found myself sleeping in my car for one night. A friend had offered me a place to stay that night, but I didn't feel at home in her house. So I said I had another place to stay and left feeling great sadness. I had no idea how difficult it is to find a place to park where you can sleep in your car. Everywhere I parked, the neighbors called the police.

So I found a less patrolled—and less safe—part of the city where neighbors were unlikely to call the police, and I dozed off and on fearing for my safety. I cried many times, wondering how people manage to sleep in their cars night after night. After that, I was offered a lovely place to stay, but I had a different view of those who live on the streets and particularly in cars. I understood how important safety is to being at home.

My refusal to stay with the friend and instead to sleep in my car revealed to me that some people don't feel at home in shelters or even in their own family's homes. Many don't feel at home anywhere. When we feel estranged, we can't say we're home. To feel *at home* includes being recognized. Without being seen, we begin to disintegrate, and our ability to think, see, hear, and function diminishes, as though we're dying. It's difficult to see yourself as whole when you're not acknowledged. How can we be brought back to life?

Offering sanctuary to those who are invisible, displaced, or discriminated against because of class, ethnicity, heritage, beliefs, race, religion, sexuality, gender, or physical ability is to respond to expressed hatred in the world. Accepting refuge in a sanctuary is a chance to reclaim who we are.

"Taking refuge" is the English translation of *sarana-gamana*; *sarana* in Pali "means shelter, protection, or sanctuary"—a place where safety and peace are possible. To take refuge in the three treasures—Buddha, Dharma, Sangha—is to follow a path that leads us home to who we are, a path of awakening.

Zen Master Shunryu Suzuki says, "We began to strive *for ourselves*, strive for God" (italics added). We reach out for love and acceptance and through practices like prayer and meditation, ceremony, drumming, and chanting, honor ourselves and evolve in a creative spiritual community. Revitalizing ourselves in community gives us the energy we need to shift our sense of who we are and transform the way we live.

Taking refuge, we gain insight and see possibilities. With the support of others, we awaken to the conditions that cause us suffering. When we say, "I take refuge," we're appealing to what brings us home to ourselves.

Tenshin Reb Anderson writes, "If taking refuge is the return flight to our own true nature, the appeal is not made to something outside ourselves nor to something inside ourselves. It is made to the great openness of being that transcends outside and inside and from which nothing is excluded."

Buddha, when he discovered that he was subject to old age, illness, and death, left his privileged home. He could no longer live in the family palace. The illusion of comfort vanished. In the sanctuary of the forest, he began to recognize a path to understand the full range of suffering and experience his connection and interdependence with others. He found a place within himself where no one is "less than" or other or invisible.

The Bible says that, in the beginning, God created heaven and earth. The earth was formless and empty, and darkness prevailed. Then there was light. Conditions changed, chaos ensued, and people were expelled from the Garden. Yet in a Zen Buddhist worldview, light and dark coexist. One does not follow the other. And everything flickers between light and dark, void and matter. This is the nature of life. Neither transformation nor chaos is random.

The movement of living beings between home and homelessness is patterned and has been systematized from the beginning of time. As expressed in Buddha's second noble truth, there are underlying causes and conditions of chaos and homelessness in all their variations. It is not by chance. And this flux is rooted in the ways we shape our lives in response to our ever-evolving needs and desires as living beings.

If we study the patterns and conditions of pervasive homelessness, we can predict the moment of the next economic upheaval, whether it's war, famine, climate imbalance, annihilation of a tribe, or other kinds of disaster. Those without resources become refugees. Over and over, impending displacements are ignored until the crisis becomes unbearable. We ignore the patterns and conditions.

Consider what was known about the levees in New Orleans before they broke in 2005 during Hurricane Katrina. What might have happened if the levees had been shored up years earlier, as had been recommended? And consider home foreclosures before the intense marketing of dangerous derivatives and mortgages to folks who could barely afford to feed themselves. When unscrupulous corporations began investing in neighborhoods, it was clear the pattern would force rents to soar, pushing out folks from their places of birth. When wild animals in surrounding woods begin to forage through our trash, we know this is a sign we will be forced to coexist. We need only look at the indicators around us to know there's about to be an upheaval.

Without examining the patterns, we continue to experience the ancient and unnecessary chaos of systemic homelessness and the consequent spiritual hunger for home. Because of chaos in our lives, we need sanctuary. I sought sanctuary from the experiences of hatred I encountered in daily living. I needed a place to meet myself upon the "return flight" to my true nature.

Ruijin, an ancient Zen master, once said, "Carving a cave of emptiness from a mountain of form leads to serenity from the ocean of misery." If we carved a cave—a sanctuary—within the mountain of misery, will our essence freely abide?

Is serenity available to all?

4

WHAT WE CREATE

Shared Community and Kinship

———•—•———

And when I lay my head down, I see the deities that blew me into existence and the winged ones who taught me to fly. I thought I was lost until I found my feathered face in you and we knew the same ancient songs. Together we felt comfort weaving what was left for us to do.

When we are homeless, we lose a way of living and the relationships that come with it.

Cultural aspects of our lives like foods, music, pastimes, customs, and traditions are lost. In sanctuary, we recover from being lost and take refuge in shared community, the collective embodiment of all that symbolizes home. And *collective* embodiment doesn't exist without *personal* embodiment and experience.

Kinship is an example of collective and personal connection. Cultural sanctuaries are based on kinships, such as race, sexuality, gender, or any combination of factors significant to feeling connected. We create a sense of love and well-being around kinship, and attend to our own and others' suffering.

Creating a sanctuary takes imagination, trust, and determination—but first it takes the courageous thought that homelessness need not be endured.

We begin by envisioning ways to foster resiliency and learn to be well while resisting injustice. We see and hear those around us who might need protective sanctuary. Artists, healers, activists, priests and priestesses, storytellers, drummers, musicians, and wisdom-keepers can help us fill the void of not belonging. We are manifesting a village in which everyone feels loved. Identity is used to empower and forge a sense of self, as a gateway to wellness in the larger world and ultimately to an experience of boundlessness and freedom.

As with everything, there is a shadow side to sanctuary. Those with intent to harm also form sanctuaries. For example, gangs establish personhood and oppressive power through the threat of violence. White supremacists create organizations to perpetuate racial dominance. Sanctuaries formed for defense or harming others arise from the same urge as sanctuaries established for healing. Well and ill sanctuaries are built upon collective pain, misperceptions, and the threat of losing home/turf/territory or losing a grip on long-held values.

Sanctuary of any kind, ill or well, can be steeped in a vat of emotions. Such emotions include:

- The need to take care of oneself and one's family
- Feelings of having been wronged
- Powerlessness
- Uncertainty
- Overwhelming fear

- Lack of patience
- Embarrassment or shame of poverty
- Lack of belonging
- Withdrawal from society
- Depression
- Loss of sense of survival

When Dr. Martin Luther King Jr. spoke of the "beloved community," it was not the first time I'd heard of such a thing. I was raised in one. Every Sunday morning, my family dressed in our finest, and we gathered with the tribe that had migrated to Los Angeles from Texas and Louisiana. We arrived in our Buicks, Lincolns, Fords, and Chevrolets. It was our time to see each other eye to eye, time to sing, to let loose from bearing yet another week of blatant discrimination.

I would be in the backseat of our Buick with my younger sister, feeling beautiful, my hair slick and wearing my shining shoes and a dress reserved for Sundays. I was headed to the beloved community where love was guaranteed.

To come to the beloved community was to head home, a place where you walk through the doors and are instantly hugged simply because you are alive. You might come to cry about what was lost or to eat homemade rolls or lemon meringue pie like they made back home. You might come to hear that song that lifts you from distress or just because you had nowhere else to go. There was nothing like listening to the old ones talk about the old times and their migration from the South in the 1940s for work. Of course they didn't always have good times, but the joy of a life gone by lit up their eyes. The memories were what they had left.

On the day Dr. King was murdered, it was clear that his call for our human connection across cultural boundaries was more than a dream. It was a prophecy.

I was in high school and students were running in the hallway yelling about the assassination. As one of few youth of color, white students looked at me as if I might attack them for what had just happened. There was a feeling that African Americans had lost the race war, but it was clear that Dr. King's dream was as lucid and prophetic as the dreams the Buddha had from which emerged the four noble truths. It was more than a dream about whites and blacks holding hands and singing, eating at the local diner, living in shared neighborhoods, or desegregating schools.

The beloved community King spoke of was meant for an entire country, an entire world, not just the black community. He was encouraging a *sanctuary* within our country and our world that would be based on peace, so we might live in the magnificent oneness available to all beings.

Although he used the language of the day, speaking to the brotherhood of "man," the patriarchy of mostly white and black men in the movement, excluding black women and black gays and lesbians, the ultimate aim of King's Southern Christian Leadership Conference was "to foster and create the 'beloved community' in America." At that time, like many times after, black people were under siege, so his language was pointedly addressed to white people, but his message—and his audience—was larger than we could imagine.

He was speaking about creating a community of peace within a country that was built on division and destruction. At the time, with Jim Crow laws in effect, the country was not safe for black people. When Dr. King called for a beloved community, he was envisioning a sanctuary for those who felt marginalized or displaced. King's sanctuary would re-establish a sense of personhood.

Although influenced by separate and unequal access to housing, education, and health care for black Americans, his call for integration was not of the relative kind. Dr. King did not imagine *only* a political and legislative response to his call for integration—he was calling for a larger and more powerful kind of integration, like Buddha's teachings of interrelationship, Thich Nhat Hanh's interbeing, or Paramahansa Yogananda, who said, "May my love shine forever on the sanctuary of my devotion and may I be able to awaken thy love in all hearts."

Dr. King said, "We are tied together in the single garment of destiny, caught in an inescapable network of mutuality." He was asking us to acknowledge that this destiny was, in fact, the very basis for our existence as a country. He was begging the nation to transform itself and begin anew.

The creation of the beloved community as a vision of sanctuary was both an action *and* a consciousness to be embodied across the globe. Beloved community as sanctuary was, for Dr. King, a heartfelt way to attend to those who did not feel at home in the U.S. and to prevent the continued killing of human life on this planet, especially black people. His call was an alarm going off, not a man dreaming in his sleep. He felt we could not go on as a society without conscious love.

We continue to experience racial and other kinds of hatred today. Is it in part because we misunderstood

Dr. King's teaching as a political ploy to give power to black people rather than as a teaching of love or interbeing?

In a beloved community, our sacred incarnation is honored and loved. In a beloved community, "unaccept-able" embodiments of the larger society are accepted. The protection, refuge, healing, guidance, and companionship found in sanctuary are prerequisites for our happiness and well-being. Finding personhood, dignity, and respect are the soil in which we can plant our feet in a true home. When all is well, home is sanctuary and sanctuary is home.

In the novel *Paradise*, by Toni Morrison, five harm-less, magic-practicing women take refuge together in a for-mer convent on the outskirts of the black town of Ruby, Oklahoma. The women become scapegoats for the town's catastrophes. In Morrison's words, they were, "throwaway people that sometimes blow back into the room after being swept out the door." The women, of various ethnicities, are perceived as threats to the town's God-given sense of morality, so the black men of Ruby come to the convent to kill them. Black men killing women of color made the novel controversial, but the story was not lost on those who understood the essence of the story—women creating sanc-tuary for their own survival.

Ironically, the town of Ruby had been created for dark-skinned blacks who were put out of towns populated pre-dominantly by light-skinned blacks. Ruby was a sanctuary for the most rejected. Likewise, each woman in the con-vent sought healing from tragedies that had taken place in their own lives in their original homes. The convent and the town of Ruby were both intended as beloved communities of peace, but when unchecked fear erupts as superiority, the quest for home must be renewed and yet another paradise must be found. This phenomenon is repeated in real life for many throughout time.

In an interview about her novel, Morrison is asked, "Why does paradise necessitate exclusion?" This inquiry leads us back to the healing qualities and purpose of sanctuary. The women in the novel simply found each other and bonded through the suffering each had endured. Together they could be free. But the men of Ruby, triggered by their own distress, displacement, and homelessness, their fear fed by puritanical and stereotypical views of *free* women, mounted violence against them. This is familiar throughout history, groups of people excluded because of fear, having to reconcile loss of kinship, language, and belonging and the pain of all that was left behind, seeking a scapegoat in others who are even more excluded.

Morrison depicts how exclusion leads us to establish sanctuary to fill the void of being uprooted, to close the gap between home and homelessness. She describes experiences of violence and isolation one can experience in one's own homeland. Displacement is historically racialized, classed, and gendered, and heaped upon the poor while others go untouched. Who has to dig through such rubble to uncover what previously represented a precious life?

Although Morrison uses *finding paradise* as a metaphor for finding home, she points to the violent acts against unwanted people and that creating sanctuary is not always a calm, sweet journey to wholeheartedness. Harmful exclusion that catalyzes sanctuary fuels a pandemic that threatens communities and nations of people. The women in the convent-sanctuary were seeking to re-establish their autonomy. They were carving out a place of serenity in the mountain of misery.

As a consequence of recent movements in America against the murder of unarmed black people by police, sanctuaries have emerged to protect and address the lives of black people. Witnessing this, I wondered, *What might a spiritual path and a protected sanctuary look like for those who suffer this kind of hatred?*

Sustenance, nurturance, and rejuvenation are certainly crucial. You might envision an intentional, inspiring, multigenerational environment inclusive of differences, especially those considered unacceptable in the larger society. Most importantly, restorative, core-healing practices would be used to navigate the world. A spiritual path and protected sanctuary for families and communities suffering brutality would be a non-oppressive, non-judgmental, and welcoming place to come home to from the front lines of fighting for human dignity.

Those who live on the margins of society will always need to find refuge that is inclusive of protest *and* wellness, resisting *and* embracing.

The black church was a sanctuary of my past. I experienced tension where I struggled with limited teachings of sin and hell that seemed absent of love. Still, the black church offered a foundation for sustaining the life of our community, our families, and our personal lives.

The church was the first place black sharecroppers and farmers went when they migrated north from the rural south. There they could find out about housing, employment, and schools where church members were teachers.

The church also was the place to receive orientation to the big city. It would have been dangerous in the 1940s, '50s, and '60s to go north and not connect with other black people. Since church was where everyone gathered, it was the place for political movements, rejuvenation, and the non-acceptance of the objectification of black people. The church was the holy ground for grieving, speaking openly, talking loud, loving hard, and disagreeing in the name of God. We could be fully ourselves.

I lost this sanctuary when I moved from Los Angeles to San Francisco.

I settled into an apartment at the foot of Twin Peaks near Golden Gate Park. My well-paid job was one bus ride straight downtown. Life was a breeze. I felt free to come and go in a strange city, making it on my own. Then, suddenly, I received a call from the minister of the Church of Christ, three miles from my house, the same kind of church I'd been raised in. My hard-to-pronounce name rolled off his tongue as if he'd said it many times before. I wanted to say that Earthlyn was not available to come to the phone, but I couldn't lie to a minister. I affirmed I was she, and he told me that my mother had asked him to check in on me.

I was so angry at her for interfering in my life, my face began to burn. I wanted to shout, "I'm a grown woman!" but the truth was I didn't want anyone back home to know I was partying in the streets of San Francisco and had gone a great distance from the church in a short time. He invited me to meet his congregation and insisted I come the next Sunday. I declined. He called again, insisting my mother needed to know I was doing well. I groaned to indicate disinterest. He called a couple more times and finally gave up, saying he was there whenever I needed him.

He never called again—and I never went to his church.

While I felt grounded in my decision not to go, years later I understood that for my mother who migrated from Louisiana to Los Angeles in 1942, the church was a crucial sanctuary for black migrants from the South. Even though I had seen many new arrivals stay at our house, it didn't cross my mind that Mom was encouraging me to attend church not for the Christianity per se, but as refuge, the way of survival for black people of her times.

What had been a refuge for my mother felt to my spirit like a prison. In my freedom, I co-created many sanctuaries for myself and others. Some were soothing, some not, depending on whether I needed that sanctuary to change or remain the same.

Change is inevitable—and so sanctuary is never a static oasis. It's a mistake to imagine that everyone in a sanctuary has the same views, even if it was shared experience that brought them together. Latecomers often have different needs than the founders, and a schism can ensue. Dissenting views can help a group grow if tended skillfully, but they often split a group apart. Financial scarcity or abundance can cause rifts, as can changes of leadership. As a community grows, some might drop out when new beliefs or protocols make them uncomfortable. Sanctuaries, however homey they might feel, are often external to the longing to be home, and as such are therefore vulnerable to dissatisfaction and dissolution.

Even a sanctuary has imperfections that mirror us, despite our ideals. When suffering arises, there is a profound opportunity for transformation if there is willingness to stay a while. We see our differences most when there is suffering in a community, and therefore acknowledging the sanctuary's shadow is a way to alleviate disappointment and clip the wings of flight during difficult times. Quaking within a sanctuary is a chance to observe, understand, heal, and be guided home to be fully who we are. Do not accept abuse, disregard, violence, or harm. But if conditions are favorable, resolving conflict is a good way to actuate connection and know yourself. Through satisfaction comes dissatisfaction; through dissatisfaction comes discontent; and discontent can bring about awakening to a boundless self that is uncaused and unconditional.

If you are still feeling the positive effects of community despite the discomfort, staying can be beneficial for cutting through harmful habits and piercing illusions. You are the judge whether you've stayed too long, don't know how to leave, or are afraid to leave. Maybe your participation has moved from aspiration to routine. Perhaps the suffering within the community paralyzes you with unexpressed grief. When much of your life has been amid systemic oppression, these are familiar responses. If the community is similar to you in terms of race, sexuality, gender, class, spirituality, or livelihood, and then "not belonging" surfaces, it can provide a tangible opportunity for transformation and healing or at minimum provide a gauge to understand how you suffer.

Discomfort in sanctuary can bring attention to the pain of not feeling kinship with those who appear as you. You recognize the bitterness that arises when you don't feel accepted, loved, or cherished. When sanctuary becomes a substitute for being mothered, cared for, or seen as worthy, you can learn from this. Notice if you are trying to sustain contentment and avoid conflict through inner censorship, not making waves, suppressing anger, or appeasing others. While freedom from the distress of homelessness is your intention when entering sanctuary, this freedom is found in understanding that you are not meant to shoulder all of your pain alone. Suffering in community can help you see what needs mending. In the safe container of sanctuary, we can become more aware of ourselves.

If a sanctuary has clear and specific values, ceremonies, or spiritual medicine, it can help us access peace and authenticity. We can witness the impact our life has on others and theirs on us. Swami Ashokananda said, "It does not matter in what state a person is, if by some means they can be made aware of their true nature, in one moment they can wake from the dream of this vicious reality. You do not have to complete the whole story of delusion or ignorance. Let the first chapter be finished. After that, why not wake up?"

Becoming aware that you have been living a story usually comes after the emotional upheaval of the heart. When enraged or grieved, take time away from the sanctuary but if you run out the door at the first sight of suffering, you might miss the opportunity to find home within chaos, turmoil, or oppression.

When we enter a spiritual path, we join the fire inside ourselves with the fire of others. The fire at the entryway tests our commitment. In indigenous traditions, we are taught that fire is the first element where ancestors reside. It is the place of illumination and purification, where prayers are made. We can either go through the fire or go back out the door until another gateway appears. But discomfort will arise again, and eventually we can choose transformation with the help of experienced teachers, gatekeepers, or deities who can guide us along.

In sanctuary, we learn that connectedness is the way home. Being connected to others, to earth, air, fire, water, and oneself is primal and it is crucial for coexistence. Some deny needing other people or communities, but even they have to rely on others for clean water and decent soil to grow food and medicinal crops. We depend on a biological interaction between two people to arrive on this planet. Self-reliance doesn't exist in the universe, where resources and strength are shared. When interdependence is ignored in sanctuary, suffering ensues. The notion of home is sabotaged when individualism overpowers communal reality.

Solo efforts toward happiness are impossible to sustain.

When Crocodiles Die is a tale I wrote years ago that illustrates the depth of our inescapable relationship with all living beings. The story takes place deep in the forest of Ankarana in Madagascar. A man named Mustafa, a descendant of the ancient Vazimba people who disappeared 2,000 years ago, paces the earth waiting for the *famadihana*, a ceremony in which his bones should be turned. But everyone who knew him, including all his relatives, are dead, and the people who now live on the land overlook his crypt whenever there is a ceremony. Each day he enters a cave where the underground river runs and crocodiles walk through mud, and he sings in the hope that the sound will help the villagers find his bones. The villagers enjoy the ancient music, but they don't search for him.

One day a gunshot rings out from the dark cave. Mustafa runs to see what has happened. A hunter has killed one of the sacred crocodiles. Mustafa begins to weep and his cries echo out from the cave into the forest. The hunter, frightened, runs from the weeping of a man he cannot see. Mustafa bends over the crocodile, whose body is covered in small jagged mountains. He has a three-foot-long head, fangs the size of an index finger, and a bullet in his skull. Mustafa says to the crocodile, "I'm sorry. The hunter has not learned." He drags the giant reptile to where the hunter is trembling on the bank of the river. Mustafa demands that the hunter look at what he has done. The hunter wants to run from the voice of the ghost, but he is drawn to the body of the crocodile. At that moment, the hunter sees the crocodile wearing his own face, and he begins to wail, understanding that he too has died. He stays at the edge of the water crying and cursing Mustafa, long enough that the flesh falls off the crocodile. The villagers hear the hunter's ghost who cries, eats dead crocodiles, and curses. They wonder what has happened to the singing.

Mustafa returns to the hunter and says, "I can help you." The hunter dries his tears and listens. "If you take care of my bones, you will live again," Mustafa tells him. The hunter agrees and asks Mustafa to show him the crypt where his bones lie. He finds the burial site, unwraps the body as instructed by Mustafa, and with great care rewraps the bones in new cloth. Mustafa is happy and begins to sing again and drums on the hollow trunks of dying trees. The villagers are happy to hear once again the music of the ancient Vazimba.

"What about me?" asks the hunter.

"You will live," Mustafa says. "Go back to the bank of the river and wait."

The hunter returns and sits silently waiting to come alive again. After two days, a village girl comes with her mother to bathe in the river. After they play for a while, the girl points and says, "Why is that man riding the back of a crocodile?" The mother looks but does not see. Suddenly the hunter is moving in the river and feels someone on his back. He looks up and sees Mustafa riding him like a horse. The hunter twists to try and bite Mustafa's leg and notices he has grown fangs as long as an index finger. He whips his new long thick tail in the water trying to break loose of having become a crocodile. Mustafa laughs as he rides the hunter through the river. When he passes the little girl and her mother, he flings the notes of the ancient songs from his heart into the heart of the little girl. From that day on, the hunter lives on as Mustafa's crocodile, and the little girl who can see ghosts begins singing ancient Vazimba songs.

Without the songs, the village had suffered and the hunter forgot that his life was connected to the crocodile, to Mustafa, and to the village, that the crocodile's life was his own. Once Mustafa's bones were settled, the hunter lived on, although in a body he didn't expect, and the villagers were able to hear their beloved songs again.

When crocodiles die, we lose, we die.

If your effort to reach home is solely personal, it is delusory. To overcome homelessness, we need each other.

Everything and everyone advances and affirms the self. Where are we from? Where are we a people? Is this our home?

We may look back on our past and forward into the future for answers to these questions, and discover that there are none.

We leave; we arrive.

There may not be visible signs telling us, "I am home" or "I have arrived," but if there are tears, breathing, and a heartbeat that signal, "I am alive," that is the door to enter.

5

TOUCHING THE MOTHER'S FEET

Understanding Our Common Birth

———•◦•———

I removed my sandals outside the ruins of an ancient temple in India. Sporting locs and sweaty brown skin, I stepped in where the door used to be and planted my feet in the mix of cow dung and mud. In the temple that had only one wall and the sky as its ceiling, I wondered what it must have been like a thousand years ago to chant there, to sit in silence listening to cow bells and wooden wagons. The crumbling limestone statue of Shakti had no eyes, no nose, and chipped lips, and yet the ripples of her presence led me to touch the Mother's feet.

At the Mother's feet, there is a sense of sanctuary, a sacredness, integrity, and purpose, the essence of one body, one landscape, and one ocean. In such a place, masks are dropped and we can wear our original faces without apology. In a liberated sanctuary, differences that are unacceptable in society are wholeheartedly embraced, creating a shelter in which all are free to be who they are given their actions are non-violent and non-harming. When distressed by homelessness, we can touch a sense of Mother and attend to the suffering of displacement and dismemberment.

Homes today, whether our physical homes or our inner, personal lives, are fragile and susceptible to destruction. The demolition begins the moment we turn away from who we are and thereby from our primal connectedness, the ancestral knowing of ourselves as communal. Disconnection leads down a path of systemic homelessness, personal and collective. Something at the core of this disconnection allows a human being to live on the streets. In a Tibetan Buddhist practice, you look at everyone as having been your mother in a past life. This is a difficult practice if you are subject to hatred by others. The teaching is espousing kindness, even toward those we find unlovable or from whom we feel disconnected. It is a practice to cultivate our coexistence as people. We can carry the sense of our common experience of having been born to access this teaching. We each have parents who gave us birth. We recognize them as the portals of our coming into being, and we touch the source of something sown deep into us that recognizes our connectedness. When we recognize our common birthing, meaningful relationship happens and superficiality wears away, and a deeper, greater love of life surfaces.

The loving-kindness sutra teaches us to love others the way a mother would risk her life to protect her only child. Each of us is capable of suffusing love throughout the world. We were all birthed from the same ancient Mother Earth. When we are blind to this Mother, not seeing that we are all her children, then we understand how homelessness is difficult to eliminate.

In Zen Buddhism, we regard ourselves as the child of Prajnaparamita, who is also known as the Mother of All Buddhas. Prajnaparamita means "the Perfection of Wisdom." We drink her milk of transcendent light, a wisdom that comes from no one and is directed toward no one. Through understanding Mother-Wisdom, the bodhisattva understands that to ease anyone's individual suffering, we must ease the suffering of all Prajnaparamita's "children." This wisdom can bring light to the suffering of homelessness.

In African spiritual traditions, the ocean is the Mother, and the deities of the ocean are Mami Wata or Yemaya. Some years ago, I experienced the power of Mami Wata directly when I danced my way into a tribe from Dahomey that had taken up residence in South Central Los Angeles. I arrived at their African restaurant on Pico Boulevard, eager to taste their "African tacos." Four lanes of cars and the Santa Monica city bus rumbled outside the storefront restaurant, which was painted light blue with a small bit of African artwork. Inside was dark and cool. It was tiny, the kitchen sat almost in the center of the dining area.

"Welcome, come on in," the sweet voice of a young African woman called, her dress the same blue as the walls.

"Thank you," I said and sat at a low table on the floor, on a pillow. There were no chairs or eating utensils. Patrons ate with their fingers. Taped music of kalimbas and drums played above my head. I ordered the tacos, filled with black-eyed peas, raw cabbage, and a spicy sweet sauce. I also ordered fried plantains and the spicy greens and fish stew.

Weeks later, I found myself eating there with the tribe at the restaurant and dancing at their ceremonies which were held in their private home. No one ever explained the tradition. Sometimes I brought my sisters. Once invited, you learn by doing, allowing whatever comes up in the ritual to be, and to dance with it. There was faith in the ceremony and nothing to question. The tribe from Dahomey had chosen me and I them. We were attached to one another without being formally introduced. The depth of our spiritual relationship became evident one night in a ceremony when, unbeknownst to me, a man had been chosen for me to marry.

The summer evening of this ceremony was hot and filled with the fragrance of jasmine. My younger sister, a friend, and I went to the house of the tribe, as we had done many times before. We'd come to dance with the people and the rhythm of the drums. We entered the large backyard filled with oak and magnolia trees, vines of white jasmine flowers, tall birds of paradise, and white calla lilies. About twenty folks lived at the house, and they were already in a circle dancing on the grass. The sun was setting above on their heads but it wasn't dark enough to me for the women to be dancing bare-breasted. I spotted neighbors in an upstairs room of their house pointing at the circle and laughing. I could only imagine what was in their minds—drums and Africans in the middle of South Central Los Angeles!

We danced into the night, going in and around in a circle, each one coming to the *Babalawo,* the head priest, prostrating in front of him and moving on. Finally, I noticed a man dancing in the center of the circle with a long stick. He would leap into the air, come down, then point the stick at someone, then move again and point the stick at someone else. Eventually, he pointed the stick at me. I kept dancing and smiling—not understanding what was going on, only that I felt at home, loving the darkness of my skin and feeling connected to the kinfolk from Africa. Then the dancing man leaned toward my ear and whispered, "You have been chosen."

"What?" I said, unable to hear well.

"You have been chosen."

"For what?" I asked.

"To be a wife. We have chosen a husband for you. Please come into the house," he said with a thick accent.

With bulging eyes, I looked around the circle and noticed that all the ones he had pointed the stick at were no longer in the circle. I looked at my sister and my friend as though I'd been told the world was round and I'd never known.

"Please," he said, "come into the house."

I looked at my sister and said, "Time to go." Then I turned to the dancing man, "It's time for me to go. Thank you," as if declining a piece of birthday cake. The man stepped back and the Babalawo glared. I had disrupted a spiritual mission. I left the yard at the beat of the drums. I was afraid that in the reverie of the ceremony, I would accept the arranged marriage. I wanted to go home to Dahomey, a place I'd never been, to be with the tribe I'd fallen in love with, but I was not ready for such a major change in my life.

The next day, I went back to the restaurant. The chosen husband, as he announced to me, was handsome, the same height as myself. He asked that I come home with them to Dahomey. He pleaded, saying I belonged to them, looked like them, and asked if I could see that. I smiled without answering. He waited on me hand and foot, feeding me and feeding me. I tried to pay for my lunch, but he refused and I walked away. How could I tell my parents, who wouldn't even eat the food because it was African, that I was marrying a stranger and would live thousands of miles away with his family for the rest of my life?

I waited a month before going back to the restaurant, hoping that they would forget about this idea of me being married to one of their tribesmen. Hunger for those African tacos, tribe, and ceremony brought me back to where I had been filled with dancing and my own darkness.

I drove up, parking the car without looking at the restaurant, because I knew where it was. But when I looked up, it wasn't there. There was no sign of a restaurant, no sign of the Dahomey tribe having been there. It was as if it had all happened in my imagination. I cried, knowing that I did want to go with them, but it didn't make sense. My fears of leaving what I knew at nineteen years of life far outweighed my stepping into a West African legacy that perhaps still awaits me.

I walked back into my parents' house that night feeling that I had missed out on being truly at home, that I had become paralyzed at a spiritual gateway. As I entered our pink Spanish Mediterranean house, I wondered if I looked different to my parents. Could they see that I'd been through an initiation, that my heart had been opened to vast new possibilities? They looked at me with no questions. Perhaps they saw the sadness that was on my face. There would be no more dancing with the people who were from the place I'd never been. But through them I connected to the possibility of my being a child of the Dahomeans and therefore having a past. I also experienced a sense of Mother-Wisdom in each of the tribespeople in their efforts to bring this Dahomean child home to cherish and protect.

The pull toward them was essential to finding home. At the ocean, I flashed on the eyes of the Dahomeans. With them I experienced having an origin that was connected to the ocean, to Mami Wata, a vastness further back than Dahomey. I learned that finding home is not abstract, not a spiritual process monopolized by religions. It's a spontaneous experience of shelter beyond the physical or the metaphysical.

Turning away from Mother-Wisdom or dishonoring others severs our connectedness and feeds homelessness. Witness the rising murder rate of homeless men and women and the increase in gated communities. We build homes and apartments with a few subsidized units to smooth over the fact that we don't provide housing for all. The true crisis is not that we don't have enough homes. It's that our hearts are closed and we're blind to the systemic patterns that lead to homelessness. We disregard particular people whose embodiment, religion, or class are different from ours, or from the dominant culture. There's a sense of entitlement among those who perceive the land as theirs and not for all the children of the world.

There are no inferior or superior existences, but many of us are confined by those who regard themselves as superior to reservations, shanty towns, slums, camps, and ghettos. How do we remain *at home*, emotionally or spiritually, with these pejorative perceptions of our magnificent lives? If we try to become something other than ourselves, our new false self can never be sustained. Assimilation and acculturation can appear helpful, but when we get too far from Mother-Wisdom, from our common birth, everyone suffers. It looks as though homelessness is happening to particular groups, but it is happening to all.

We are in a free fall toward the unknown. Our whole species is faced with homelessness. We don't know if the Earth will remain habitable for humans. Some say that we will eventually remember to return to nature. Some say we *are* nature and have never left. I believe we will return, full cycle, to circumstances where we'll be forced to live simply and close to the earth.

We need to limit our individual desires and return to a communal lifestyle to remain on the planet, or accept inevitable extinction. We need to reconnect with our ancestors and Earth as our common mother. Ancient wisdom teachings reside within us. Our minds have forgotten, but our bones know the way. If we let the intelligence of our bodies lead us, as we were led into this world at birth, we will remember the mother's milk of transcendent luminosity, the wisdom that comes from no one and is directed toward no one.

6

BROUGHT FROM
AN OLD PLACE

The Earth as Home

I rise to that which I am called to do, have agreed to do. I sit upon the earth, among trees, breath rising and falling like those who have come before me. I plant my feet in the dirt and remember how to live without feeling terrified. I let ancestors take me up with them on horses and ride bareback to ceremony learning not to be an alien in a place I came from but blend back into the dirt, fiercely and fearlessly knowing that which brought me here will take me home.

The night descended upon my face, and there was no pushing it back. The walls of the tent appeared thinner and thinner as moonlight made its way over the tops of the redwoods. There was just enough light and stillness for me to contemplate the question, "When did I become so afraid of the darkness from which we were all brought forth?" As I drifted off to sleep, the vision quest became a metaphor for living life with all its light and all its darkness. This quest would challenge my faith and place my odyssey right in the thick of what I feared most. Would I be able to find home?

A vision quest is an earth ritual for reconnecting to home, a meditation for relearning how to be at home. Going outside the temple walls and touching the earth is a practice I embarked upon many years ago, and it led me to a path of reconciliation with ancestral homelessness. This time, I committed to being in the forest for three days.

As I set up my tent, I placed African fabric and a Lakota prayer shawl on my corner of the forest floor. I created shrines of cowrie shells, a beaded white necklace, pine branches, a small bowl of water, stones, leaves, and a statue of the Buddha, and sat down to listen and to feel, slipping easily into an ancestral memory of being barefoot on my homeland.

I was like a fish in water. I could feel an ancient existence within my body, an old African woman filled with wisdom, knowing the mountains, the forest, and the animals. I felt completely at home, and I began to pray, meditate, and chant. I relished the time. I walked the earth around my tent, feeling ordinary and at the same time, filled with the presence of the talking creek and the wind rushing over my head. I stayed sitting alone, as darkness began to gather around me. I slipped into my tent and no matter how alone I felt, every crackling of the branches and crunching of dried leaves reminded me I wasn't alone. Paying full attention to my own being, possibilities of living a full life surfaced.

Then anxiety arose.

I tossed and turned fighting the feeling of being lost in this natural habitat of living beings, and I fell asleep grow-ing increasingly uncomfortable in my return to the forest. Nothing prepared me for the barking and screeching of unknown creatures, for being awakened by the scream of a hawk begging me to take flight. I had no preparation for the pounding of my heart playing the all-too-familiar rhythm of fear and no preparation for the loud rush of wildlife.

Beneath the discomfort was a lack of remembering the ancient experience of living outdoors among living beings. As a species, we feel protected by brick and mortar, yet even with the many locks on our doors and a sense of false security being inside, the disconnect from knowing our bodies as nature and nature as our home means that we live in constant fear, and eventually we are no longer home and no longer in touch with our bodies.

Our homes—and our bodies—have survived horrendous destruction. When home is invaded, it is a bitter violation of our own selves, because our true physical homes *are* our bodies. This is what we feel when someone breaks into our house and steals. It's as if we've been punched in the gut. When our bodies and our homes are not safe, we detach from any sense of being home. What would it be like if we returned to knowing nature as our home and our bodies as nature? What if our bodies *were* the vast outdoors that we've become afraid to experience?

My fear lifted as the sun rose and bird songs filled the air. I welcomed the first light on the valley floor silhouetted by redwood trees, scented by fresh pine dew, and nourished by a breakfast of hot water, lemon, honey, and red pepper. Rubbing the elbow of a madrone, I felt as though I were soothing my own great-great-grandmother.

In daylight, I sat happily among my colorful fabric hanging from the trees around my area. I prayed at the medicine wheel created with a vision quest helper, and did slow full prostrations toward the shrines I had erected on each side of the entry to my tent. I had nowhere to go, nothing to do, and no one to be for anyone else. I sat near my shrines breathing in and out for hours. If you sit alone on the earth long enough, the pain will come.

What I heard that day was an old story. For years I'd held deep feelings of remorse for not having taken care of my parents when they were old and ill. My younger and older sisters still lived in Los Angeles, and they did most of the work. I would visit for a week often to give my sisters a break, but I felt guilty for not doing more. After Mom and Dad died, I held onto the sense that I was a "bad" daughter who hadn't done enough.

After sitting for two or three hours reliving this story and trying to let it go, I suddenly heard heavy footsteps behind me. The steps came closer, and I stiffened. I didn't want to turn around. It was daytime, I thought, why should I be afraid? I sat still, slowed my breathing, and I felt some-one standing at my back. I inhaled and asked without turn-ing, "Who is it and what do you need to tell me?"

I had prayed and prepared for the presence of ances-tors, so I suppressed any fear at hearing the voice. I asked the question again and paused for an answer. "Who is it and what do you need to tell me?"

I heard what felt to be my mother's voice. She said, "I miss you and I love you."

I began to cry. I muttered that I missed and loved her too. The tears came long and hard, because I had all the time and privacy in the world to release this long-held pain. I knew this was the end of holding on to the story of neglecting my elderly parents. The past didn't matter to her and now, it no longer mattered to me.

This is how the earth heals.

The earth gives you time to breathe; the aloneness gives you the privacy to expose yourself to yourself and discover a true home within yourself and in nature. You can feel the earth holding you like a mother holding her child.

By the end of the third day, I realized that the depth of the fear I'd felt was an indication of the gap between the earth and me. When fear arises, it indicates a disconnection from home and the need for sanctuary. Perhaps the first time I experienced this was my mother's fear, which I must have felt while inside her womb, her exile from the red dirt she'd grown up with surviving the South. Perhaps the fear goes back further, to when my African ancestors were taken from the bush of home and brought to a new land. Regardless of the source, many of us are disconnected from the earth beneath our feet. I sat with this, feeling the healing of lineage take place inside me—for my great-great-great grandparents.

I stood up, having communed with ancestors who had been crying for my attention for decades, and left the quest aware of the extent to which I'd become alien to the beings of the forest, vowing to end this separation and regain a sense of belonging to the web of life. As I lifted my belongings to carry out of the forest, I remembered what I'd heard the wind say, *"Be divine in your own way. Listen, and you will know."*

Whenever I reconnect with the earth or the ocean, life's vastness returns. When difficulties come my way, I know that a prayer to be home is being answered. I've learned to stand sure-footed as life unfolds. When I feel limitations based on remembrances of things past, I see the flight of the hawk, and limitations vanish. With closure comes a new opening and a celebration of life that feels as though it could last the rest of my days. Vision quests, or any time in nature, can be a mirror reflecting light back to our most powerful and most vulnerable places. We feel invincible *and* afraid. The unsettling noises in the dark forests of our lives are cries for wellness and protection. If we listen long enough, we recognize the rumblings of the forest as the advent of transformation.

Over the centuries, our fragmented human condition has cultivated oppressive systems of living that thrive on our displacement and disconnection from each other and from the earth we tread upon. The foul and stagnant stench of injustice makes us ill. On a spiritual quest, we begin to recognize all living beings as our relatives; only then can we be in honest, wholehearted relationships with one another.

In the solitude of a vision quest, we *enter* the mysterious darkness and discover home. Facing and being intimate with the mystery is a path of engagement that includes all the world's creatures. A quest deep in nature was necessary to see the distortions that had formed in me by systemic oppression and to recognize that acceptance of what I found in my own depths had to be the first step for re-engagement with others.

Through the practice of sitting meditation, I've learned that a deep connection to the earth as home is the result of awareness *and* intimacy. Meditation brings us close to the heart. There is a natural process from awareness to intimacy to being engaged in a way that creates sanctuary and home. We can be aware of the general human condition of suffering but not necessarily intimate with the suffering in and around our personal lives, our personal homelessness. When we come to know our lives with such intimacy, we embark upon awakening. Intimacy in the context of the earth as home means acknowledging *all* the suffering and living as close as possible to that which hurts.

When we lack intimacy with our environment, we act *upon* homeless conditions externally, rather than stopping to assess the beliefs that produced these conditions. We build shelters and subsidized housing to ward off hopelessness in lieu of revamping the system of values that created it. We become increasingly violent, which fuels homelessness. Our charity is empty if it is not intimate with the suffering of disconnection.

Zen Master Dogen uses the term *shinzo*, "ever intimate." When we are ever intimate with the tensions between personal and collective suffering, we experience liberation, enlightened to who we are as human beings. A true spiritual and social justice brings light, or enlightenment, to the truth of our intimacy with each other. If only one person is suffering or one indigenous place in the world is being lost, we *must* act to save this home we all live in.

My father, who was sixty years older than I, taught me about how and where we used to live as human beings. When he sat and stared off into space, I would ask, "Daddy, what are you thinking about?" He would drop his head, look at me, and say with his thick Creole tongue, "I am looking way back." He said he was thinking about Opelousas, where he would ride his horse as he worked the land. His mother, he said, would rest on the porch of their small house and smoke her pipe. Living his days in the rural landscape taught him more than I could ever learn in our urban environment. It gave him perspectives on life that were connected to the earth. I longed for a life like his, so when I received the invitation to the vision quest, I said yes. I wanted to take the time to "look way back," as my father had so often.

From then on, every time my father told stories of his home, my feet touched the prints he'd left. His stories were not rehashing memories; they were transmitting light, a father-to-daughter transmission like the warm-heart-to-warm-heart transmission between master and student in Zen training. It took my dad a great amount of meditation and stillness to sift his stories, as I experienced on the quest. He had to distill what was important and useful until his stories were clear enough to pass on. Sitting at his feet, I could listen to his teachings day in and out. He was standing high on his mountain, sharing all he had seen in his life. I bow to him for teaching me to plant my own feet on the earth to which I shall some day return.

When the hawks scream, it calls us back to earth as our home. Without intimate engagement with the earth, we cannot be present to the people around us.

We cannot know how they are doing.

We do not see them.

When the hawk calls, we see.

7

WHERE THERE IS ENOUGH
AIR TO BREATHE

Impermanence and Home

———◆·◆———

*Death felt closer than the earth. The swing was the
perfect place in the sun for a girl who would some day
vanish. The dirt and rocks beneath her could be stud-
ied and, if necessary, spoken to. The playhouse built
by my father's hands stood in one corner of the yard,
and yet I didn't linger in it, because there wasn't
enough air to breathe and I could not feel the friend-
ship of the wind in my aloneness. So I lived on my
swing, legs flying free, where the wind could give me a
push, forever.*

Struggles with homelessness and the search for sanctuary
are intertwined with death. When a relative dies, you might
need to sell the house. When some people shop for a home,
they consider whether it's a place they can see themselves
dying in. Death from natural disasters, climate change, or
political coups can transform home. Before we die, we want
to connect with our family home one more time. We want
to say yes to these questions at our death: Was I fed by this
home? Was it a warm home? Was I welcome?

As a young girl living with God, I would daydream, especially while the rest of the family was preoccupied with television. I would enjoy being lost in space for as long as I could. While sitting still, I'd say a prayer without knowing it was a prayer. And sometimes I would sit in the bedroom I shared with my younger sister, lights out and unable to see. The longer I'd sit and gaze into space, the more I could feel the blood pumping through my body. Then suddenly, I would freeze with fear, realizing that I would some day decompose. I was scared knowing there will be death and yet not much was being done about how we lived—struggling for this and that. I was scared being in the world not knowing if I would feel at home before I died. Dehumanizing experiences in the context of life's impermanence made finding home urgent.

As a Christian, I was taught that the true home was heaven, but a place that required you to die before you could get there was not all that inviting. And knowing, even with certainty, of the existence of heaven did not calm the rage of living in a dark body in America. Praying my way through life as a way to cope with the truth of struggling as a black person and then dying became a solution in my young mind. Through prayer, my body would become the *place* where I sought peace. Seeking peace *within,* I've lived most of my life outside of my raced, sexualized, and gendered body. This non-paranormal, yet out-of-body experience has been triggered off and on by the shock of mistreatment.

In an effort to find home within my body I traveled, oddly, to Tamil Nadu, India instead of Africa. I believed that there, amid the red dirt, lush green vegetation, humid heat, and thatched roofs, I could learn something that would help me understand my life in the U.S. I went, along with a group from graduate school, to Auroville, an experiment in human unity established by followers of the Indian mystic Sri Aurobindo. Auroville's early French and German settlers joined with native Tamils to create a spiritual oasis near the Bay of Bengal. Many of the white settlers built homes and stayed in Auroville, living among the Tamils and pursuing the dream of a place where people from around the world might transcend racial, social, and religious differences and devote themselves to "the practice of divine consciousness." It was this philosophy that drew me to such a place as a sanctuary and a refuge to reflect on my life back home.

Three months after making the decision to go, our group landed in Madras, now called Chennai, the capital of Tamil Nadu state and the fourth-largest city in India. At the airport, we were surrounded by faces many shades darker than mine. Some were so black they disappeared against the dark night and all you could see were their eyes. Meeting their stares, it felt as though I was looking into midnight, and the darkness comforted me; I felt a part of the landscape.

Delirious from twenty hours of travel, we packed into a small bus, our luggage tied to the roof, for a four-hour ride down bumpy roads at high speeds, dodging trucks whose horns were blaring. Out the window I saw a gathering of men wrapped in cloth, a small candle lighting their faces as they drank from cups. For a split second, I expected to see a trash fire in the center of the circle, but these were not homeless men in an Oakland alley. This is India, I thought. It was dawn on a breezeless December morning, already ninety degrees outside.

Later I learned that in small-village life, morning is a special time for men to gather, drink tea, bathe near temple waters, and pray. The women prayerfully drew artistic *kolams* (flower designs, symbols of auspiciousness) in front of their homes to protect their families, gathered water in large urns, prepared breakfast, bathed, and went to the temple mid-morning.

Even in my first hours in India, I could feel in my bones the spirit of my African ancestry. I lay on my hard bed with candles flickering light on the walls, my body exhausted, my mind racing with excitement, and I fell asleep to the rhythm of croaking frogs. It felt like I had died and gone to heaven the Christian ministers of my childhood spoke of.

I was home.

I awoke the next morning to Tamil music from the loud-speakers of a nearby village, the Muslim call to prayer nearby, and strange, loud bird-calls. I watched dark-bodied Tamil men and women move effortlessly in the humid vapors, washing, cooking, digging, sweeping, doing things for us, in much the same way that black people in America do.

Was servitude the inevitable plight of dark people around the world?

One afternoon, as vegetables were being sautéed for lunch, I lounged in the silent shadows of the thatched-roof patio, savoring sweet black tea as I took in the vivid greenness of my surroundings. A breeze smoothed my brow. A young Tamil woman floated by and peered into my face. I remembered her from the day before and the day before that. Her long, thick tail of hair swayed as she passed by. I nodded hello. She smiled at me while carrying a basket of dirty laundry. We had no common language, but I felt a strong connection to her because of the darkness of our skin and her destiny of servitude tied to it. I jumped up to grab the basket that included my laundry. "I can wash my own," I said. She shook her head, and we played tug-of-war with the basket for some time. I didn't want a black woman being a servant to me, given the many black women in my life who had been forced to do other people's laundry to survive. She smiled and forced me to give in. Later, we became friends.

On the day I left India, I stood alongside a lake, faced the sun, and prayed. Although I'd never been there before, the body of water felt familiar. I offered gratitude for experiencing peace, feeling at home, and connecting to my soul in Tamil Nadu. I'd always imagined this happening in Africa (where I had never been) and not in this other ancient land on which my feet were constantly covered in red dirt.

Reentering the U.S., I felt lost.

I'd become used to the quiet of rural Auroville and lost sense of jumping into a car, going to the grocery store, or using a washing machine. I longed to go back to showering outdoors, riding on the back of a moped, and sitting in the middle of the road with friends on hot nights. I wanted to return to walking amid crumbling temples and sitting with hundreds of seekers at spiritual talks on the open grass.

The "me" before going to India had died.

A friend suggested I undergo a "soul retrieval" ceremony. She said I'd left my soul in India, and I knew she was right. But I wanted my soul to stay in India, the place where I first experienced freedom within the confines of my dark body, so I was slow to return to the present disconnection of body and mind from spirit. Recognizing that the chaos of my life had been longstanding, I chose to stay in

America, where my feet were planted, but under the influence of India. My time in India revealed to me that a racialized, sexualized, and gendered body can itself be a place for creating sanctuary, and that can take place anywhere—if the conditioned self dies and makes space for a new way of being in the world.

After my travels to India, after my American way of being died and a new self was born, I discovered that my spiritual path mimics my physical life and vice versa. Whether and how I am reborn is subjective and relational to my spiritual path. But we can say that there is birth and death, and that a spiritual path begins and ends in our bodies.

The body begins its decline at birth. During our lifetime—that brief period between birth and death—many of us feel betrayed by our bodies. One place we may feel this is in its gradual decline, which can give us a sense of being homeless. If my body is not what I'd like it to be, dwelling within its confines is a struggle. What can we do to make peace with the body's changes and its natural flow toward death, which means leaving our worldly home and going to a place we're uncertain of?

What can the body teach us about home, or sanctuary?

Both are impermanent.

In fact, all homes are impermanent, making homelessness, spiritually and physically, part of life's organic evolution. Everything and everyone experiences change, while the unconditioned heart remains resilient, always capable of feeding the hunger to be home. Knowing tragedy and loss are a natural part of the body's cyclical existence, we see that consciousness is not confined to our body and finding home is not dependent on form.

When I was young, I would hear older people say they feel younger than their age, and I wondered why. Now I'm their age, and I see that while my flesh is dropping away from my skeleton, my heart remains as vibrant as ever, fueled by energy beyond the physical. We can experience home even as the body deteriorates, even while losing our most basic home. If our house catches fire, our heart does not burn away too. We might temporarily feel heartbroken, but our heart will repair itself when we realize that home has not completely disappeared, only shifted. It might take time while we attend to the pain, but we can for the time being enter a sanctuary we create, or one that appears and heals. And if we are lucky, this sanctuary might become our next home.

If you are living in a body that society deems unacceptable, it can be difficult to notice the sanctuary that emerges through pain and suffering, or trust that sanctuary can appear within the fire of the hatred directed at us. Lost in the wilderness, we find it difficult to trust any spiritual practice that teaches finding home within. Ancestral displacement compounds the sense you'll never arrive home. How do we go from disheartenment to the wholehearted cultivation of home?

First we must attend to the trauma and stress of having had to live dispirited, and ask for support. Acknowledging that we are not alone in the experience of disregard, we can be assisted in the effort to cultivate home. Begin with this body, this life. If you have taken on a spiritual path, the moment of homelessness is the crucial time to rely on the wisdom of the teachings. Take refuge in what and who teaches you, the teachings, and in the community in which you practice.

You may want to have a home as your parents did, live in it with your children and grandchildren, and pass it down to the next generation. But what if your children die first or your home burns to the ground or there isn't enough money to keep the family home? You may feel enraged or sad that you've lost your property, your territory, your dream. Losing your family home, having your land stolen or occupied by others, being deported, or being taken to a new land as a slave are horrendous experiences. The impact of such losses cannot be underestimated or spiritually bypassed, even with the teaching of the true home within. They must be considered as part of the whole of life.

True home is not an object to acquire or item to check off a to-do list. Nor is it a marker of enlightenment. Our true home is in this moment, and this moment is passing and we are changing. If there were no change, none of us would have come into being. Home is a groundless force of nature that transforms our existence. It might appear that some people are stable in their homes while others are not. In fact, neither is stable. True home is impermanent. It cannot be possessed. Only a home that comes into being, arises, and ceases to be is a true home. The Earth displays its ever-evolving nature, making any home momentary. Right now I am *home* and *at home* internally, but if this experience is based on an external condition, the experience of home can disappear at any moment.

For millions of years, change has dissolved bricks, cracked stucco, rotted wood, destroyed walls, and eroded mud and straw. Yet we continue to take refuge in churches, temples, mosques, synagogues, sweat lodges, monasteries, caves, sacred circles, front porches, backyards, kitchens, jungles, rivers, oceans, mountains, and meadows.

Within these sacred spaces, our inner voice speaks to our restlessness, addressing the frustration of a never-ending struggle to arrive at the place we envision. What we feel, think, observe, and respond to while living between the cracks of freedom, within the brutal honesty of impending death, creates the sanctuaries we need.

According to many sages, we have nowhere to go and nothing to do. We are nobody, aimless—a *Dharma bum*—to borrow Jack Kerouac's phrase. It doesn't necessarily mean living in the streets without possessions. It means living fully and wholeheartedly wherever you find yourself.

We don't necessarily know who we will become in the ever-changing home. In space, a moment could be a second or it could be seven years. No matter the relative time, we live in that space. And as we live in spacious time, we experience, wherever we are, an unseen, formless place, and yet there is form and there is home. By its nature, home is bound to all other things, hence the experience of home is as eternally transient as our lives.

To survive the loss of a home, we can water the seeds of compassion in our consciousness.

As the daughter of a sharecropper's son and granddaughter of a child slave, I hold my rage with compassion. As someone who has experienced insurmountable suffering, I water the seeds of compassion within me to understand my ever-evolving home in this moment.

There is no failure or success, just a capacity to see through the eyes of impermanence.

When I am able to do so, all of life is home.

8

WHERE BAMBOO SINKS ITSELF INTO YOU

Establishing Sanctuary from a Place of Freedom

No one can guide you into your dark, moist interior, where moss has grown in layers, where bamboo could sink itself into you. Your innermost earth neither speaks with words, thinks, or takes action. Instead, it leads you mysteriously to the familiar rhythms within. Eventually you will go into your life unafraid, feeling into the dark, knowing that your heart is open.

In a famous story from the *Book of Serenity*, the Buddha was walking with the assembly of monks. He pointed to the ground, and said, "This spot is good for building a sanctuary." Indra, emperor of the gods, stuck a blade of grass in the ground and said, "The sanctuary is built." The Buddha smiled.

On another occasion, the Buddha spread his hair to cover mud and offered flowers to Dipankara Buddha. Pointing to where the hair was spread, he said, "A sanctuary should be built in this place." An elder, known for his wisdom, placed a marker in the spot and said, "The building of the sanctuary is complete." The gods scattered flowers and praised him.

It doesn't take a Buddha to establish a sanctuary.

It can be brought into being by ordinary people who have broken through the compartments of their minds. It is under our feet right now, but it takes effort to realize. We sense it in our bones but spend much time looking for it. Our first impulse is to investigate the world to find soft soil in which to plant the self. There is only one thing more fascinating than the self; it is the world in which self lives. But if we *only* look at the world, we lose sight of who we are and forget where we'll actually find soft soil. Since we don't grow in isolation, looking at the world and how we are conditioned by it is a prudent step in finding sanctuary.

In a course I taught on how we are shaped, I gave the students one question each week, such as these:

How are you conditioned by your family's beliefs and values? How have you taken on the behavior of your peers or friends? How have you become your religion or spiritual path? In what ways has the society informed your existence?

The intended outcome is self-discovery, realizing that conditioning is a necessary part of growing. We do not grow independently. Yet, with a consistent chosen path, we can leave behind the reflexes of our conditioning, act from a mature mind and heart, and become more able to participate in our destinies. What might be your unique vision for sanctuary that is not trapped in habits, opinions, beliefs, prescriptions, or standards of your upbringing? What have you agreed or disagreed with that smothered your creative fire in establishing sanctuary?

In the traditional Christian perspective, death is the price we pay for the original sin of Adam. We are offered resurrection if we live the will of God. But even with that offer, I felt doomed. I didn't know if I could be forever "good," as I understood God's desire for me, so I accepted the symbolic ritual of resurrection and at age eleven, I decided to be baptized. I needed something to hold me through the pain and suffering of being a black girl child. I said to my younger sister, "It's time for us to be buried in the blood of Jesus." She was willing to do whatever I said, because if she didn't, I would make her do it anyway.

Tyranny can be effective if you are afraid of living your truth alone.

I convinced her of *her* sins. I never revealed that I needed her more than she needed me. "Now, remember, when they ask why you want to be baptized, say 'For the remission of my sins.'" I'd been listening Sunday after Sunday for the right words.

"Re-*what*?" she asked.

I worried. Would they believe this eight-year-old girl?

"Come with me when they call the souls to Christ." She looked confused. She never actually said yes, but I insisted she come with me whether she could say *remission* or not.

That great Sunday arrived. The sermon was almost over, and I told my mother, "We're going to get baptized." Her eyes filled with tears of joy. She had few such moments, so I was pleased. I floated above my seat for a second and came down softer and kinder than the day before.

I turned to my sister and whispered in her ear, "It's time to go."

As the congregation sang to bring souls to Christ, my mouth went dry. I grabbed my sister's hand as if leading her to her righteous destiny, but I was dragging my own insecurity with me, heading for eternal life through baptism.

We tiptoed down the aisle, big white satin bows around our hot-curled ponytails, one on each side of our heads. I shouldn't have looked back, but I did. I saw a million faces singing and smiling at us, and as my heart sank into my belly, I grabbed my sister and ran us back to our seats. Abort mission. Too many people looking at us.

"We'll try again next Sunday," I told my sister, watching my mother's mouth quiver. The happy tears were gone.

My sister agreed to try again, looking at me as if to ask what is it that we're trying to accomplish? I didn't know how to explain to her that this was a way to save ourselves from the hell of being black.

The next Sunday we walked up to the front of the church. I didn't look back. We repented for our childhood sins. Mine were stealing cookies from hidden places in the house, eating all the vanilla ice cream, stealing the tiny pink, sweet children's Bayer aspirin and then lying about it. We were instructed to put on white gowns. As we got closer to the baptismal pool, the water looked higher than I had imagined. Neither of us could swim. I held down the sense that perhaps we should wait. We were too close. There was one boy before me and then we would be dunked in the water and resurrected.

The singing grew louder.

A brother of the church reached out for my small hand. I couldn't quite grab his big hands so he lifted me like a baby. I was eleven but I looked seven. He sat me down on a brick in the freezing water, said the words, "In the name of the Father, the Son, and the Holy Ghost, I now baptize you," and down I went.

The water went right up my nose and I embarrassingly choked. He lifted me up and out like a wet rag doll. It happened so quickly I wanted a second dunk to make sure I'd be cleansed of the hurt, pain, and deceptions of life.

One of the church sisters grabbed me so I could get dressed. Although I didn't see my sister's water burial and resurrection, I imagined her balled up like a wet black cat.

That was it. We were baptized. Reborn. In the evening, watching *Bonanza* on TV, I contemplated ending sucking my thumb, the most radical act I could do for peace. It was time to grow up and save the world from itself. There was no time to waste. I had been born and I was surely going to die.

The next day, I expected to be loved by the world because I was a good human living the will of God. But that Monday morning we were still poor, black, pleasured by freshly cut St. Augustine grass, black walnut ice cream, still wishing for a life that never ended.

In the relative plane of existence, birth has a before and after as well as death. In the absolute dimension, time is continuous, not sequenced in the way we usually perceive it, and there is no birth and no death, only time itself. Given that the existence of God remained in my heart, this was difficult to digest.

The Christianity I grew up with offered a supervised world in which God was in control. The Buddha's teachings offer freedom in which life extends throughout the ten directions of the universe. *Zazen,* Zen meditation, is not a method by which one reaches awakening, but is itself awakening. When one practices zazen, there is an unfolding of self-liberating awakening that is continuous and undying. Both religious experiences shaped who I am, and left me with questions about the truth of who I really am. My desire is to know God, which is to know love.

Swami Abbhutananda said, "The true being is ever free, ever pure, and remains untouched by good or evil." In the realm of the absolute, good and evil are merely walls of the mind. According to author and Buddhist scholar Charles Johnson, "In the realm of relative truth and contingency, of conditioned arising, each person presents to us a phenomenal, historical 'substance,' which due to custom and habit we refer to as individuality"—this is the conventional truth in which incarnation is historically conditioned and we see ourselves as that conditioning.

Over the years I had conjured up a life of reverence, peace, poetry, tea, esoteric teachings, painting, and sacred conversations with others about life, being born, being a daughter, and living in a dark body. In what environment would such freedom exist where I am ever free while also being subject to the duality of life?

Have you ever heard of a Japanese samurai being reincarnated as a black woman? That would be me.

My best act of magical blackness was to test the freedom of the teachings as a way to loosen the grip of oppression. To enter the Japanese-based Zen world and be ordained as a priest was an Afro-futuristic detour from what I expected for a second chance at resurrection. It was to take the diverse aspects of my blackness and create a galaxy that had the known and the unknown in it. It was to become, in my own way, the black Catholic nun I spotted as a child walking in our neighborhood.

Several events led to my ordination.

One such event was an interview to be approved to do a solo retreat at the Vedanta Retreat Center in Olema, where you receive a free cabin in the woods to practice silence. I met a Swami in San Francisco and sat before him in my corporate clothes and my stylish leather briefcase in hand.

I was in a hurry to get back to work, and he asked, "How are you?"

"Fine," I said, as fast as possible while checking my watch.

I sat in his small office, remaining as still as possible so as not to accidentally bump knees. He asked again, "How are you?" When he repeated himself, I knew he wanted a different answer. I became quiet and still, looked deep into his eyes, and to my surprise said, "I'm tired."

My briefcase fell onto the floor. He looked at me. I wanted to look away because I had never been in the presence of anyone who looked with the eyes of unconditional love. It was the look a child seeks in the eyes of her mother—to be loved no matter what.

Tears welled up, and I continued to look.

He bowed his head as if to pray for me. "When you go on retreat you cannot write or read books," he said. I smiled, because it meant I was approved to go but I had never gone away without writing or reading. What would I do?

He said, "I want you to focus on your spiritual practice. I want you to be in silence."

"But I chant," I said. In fact, I had been chanting like a maniac.

"Only silence, no chanting," he said.

The interview lasted ten minutes.

I arrived at the retreat center and unpacked my clothes, a book, and a journal. I sat on my bed contemplating whether to disobey him by reading and writing. Then, I opened the curtains to my room. White deer sat in the grass two feet from my cabin. Amazed at how comfortable the deer appeared, I sat on the steps and began breathing with them. It deterred any further thoughts of reading or writing. They taught me how to sit and listen in the quiet of the land. The trees breathed with us under a canopy of blue sky. Although similar to my state of mind just before I wrote poetry, it was a new kind of silence that held renewal, rest, and a gateway to meeting a self beyond all life experiences.

After an hour, I grabbed a sweater and decided to take a walk.

My new deer family did not move as I crossed over long narrow legs and muddied hoofs. Heading up a small grassy hill, I remembered the caretaker warning me that there were hundreds of acres and I could get lost. I sat down on a hill not far from my cabin, and for an hour I just looked out into the distance. Then I decided to challenge the fear of being lost. I stood, inhaled, and took off deep into the woods. After just a few minutes, I felt fear taking over. My heart raced, and I was even startled by the flutter of humming-birds. Then I remembered the deer, unafraid, and knew that the bears I imagined mauling me were only in my mind. I continued in silence. I had never been in the woods alone or even sequestered away from the chaos of the world.

The silence grew on me. The swaying of trees never seemed so majestic. The sun had never felt the way it was that day, setting alongside me rather than being overhead. I sensed small animals lurking in the bushes. The whipping of snakes on dry leaves startled me. I had an urge to talk about what I was feeling, but fortunately there was no one to break the journey of discovering sanctuary.

For three days I sank into the abyss of nature.

I knew nothing about formal meditation at the time, and did not focus on what the mind or the breath was doing. The silence I experienced was just that, silence. Not a word. Thoughts rose and fell like waves in the ocean. I turned inward and the doors of my heaven were opened. I needed only to walk in. I became intensely interested in living from a place of silence and intimacy, a place I begin to call a spiritual life. I had allowed silence to be spiritual medicine rather than the coping skill I learned as a child who wanted to be invisible in her dark skin.

The swami's guidance of silence was an immeasurable gift.

After many return trips to Vedanta Retreat Center for solo retreats, I met two Zen priests. They impressed me by the way they used their breath to present their teachings. I could see that their steady gaze and still bodies came from the place of medicinal silence I'd experienced at Vedanta. Zen was breathing and therefore a body practice. I needed to breathe in a way I could be brought back to a natural presence of well-being, home to my body, which had suffered from its darkness.

"I have to go stay at San Francisco Zen Center for a while. Three weeks, that's all," I said to my beloved. She cried. We had just come together as a couple, a journey that was both sweet and horrendously difficult. Our friends and family couldn't help us. We were alone. We needed each other, but I couldn't stay home.

"I have to find out the reasons for my suffering, the reasons I harm myself and others. I hope you understand. I can't suffer like this any longer," I said.

I began packing my things into boxes, temporarily moving out of the apartment we'd just moved into. Mexican music thumped loudly from the streets through our walls, audible throughout the Fruitvale section of Oakland. As it grew louder, I didn't know what to say because I wasn't sure what I was doing. I threw into the boxes a few books, enough underwear for a month so I wouldn't have to wash, and black clothes because that's what they wore there. Conveniently, my closet had mostly black clothes. I'd been wearing black since I was thirteen, as though I'd been preparing for Zen training since then. I looked back into the apartment, not knowing if I'd return. I always held open that a spiritual journey could steer me anywhere. Perhaps my beloved knew I might not come back and if I did, I might not be the same person. Something of Zen might take me over in the way the music from the streets filled our space of departure.

We rode to the center in silence; the feeling between us was stiff. We both had been taught the deep medicine of Congolese drum medicine. Wasn't that enough? We'd sat in the heat of a Native American sweat lodge, singing prayers. Would those prayers hold us? We watched cars racing by. Where did I think I was going? Perhaps I should have been yelling to stop the car, but that didn't happen.

Forty minutes later, we arrived at the front steps of San Francisco Zen Center at Page and Laguna, after flying across the Bay Bridge.

My heart pounded. Surely I was desperate. It felt as though I was delivering myself to an insane asylum because I had gone crazy from the doings of life.

At the top stairs in her robes stood the Zen teacher who would be leading the three-week intensive. She had a beautiful, warm smile. Why is she waiting outside? Is she waiting for me? How can I sneak in with her standing there? Why is she smiling? I smiled back, thinking, *Why am I smiling!?—I can barely breathe.*

The teacher helped carry my boxes and luggage up the stairs. "So glad to have you Earthlyn," she said.

Tears welled up in my beloved's eyes. The teacher noticed and intuitively surmised that my beloved was struggling with my leaving the world for three weeks.

But she had not lost me to Zen Center—she had lost me to the discovery of myself. The teacher assured her they would take good care of me and give me back. More tears from my beloved.

She intuitively knew I wouldn't come back as who I was. I could only imagine a voice in her head saying, "Who will she be?"

I whispered in her ear, "If I do this, we will have a better life together," not knowing if it was true. It sounded good and likely. I dropped my head, ashamed of leaving her so soon in our relationship. I could have apologized, but that wouldn't have been honest.

I needed to be at the asylum; I needed help.

We stood in the lobby for some time. When my beloved turned to leave, I wanted to ask her to stay longer, but I didn't. If she stayed I might gain some sanity and follow her out the heavy front doors. I gave her a weak smile—or more precisely a guilty-for-leaving one. She hadn't signed up for this.

We said goodbye and slowly she left. The deed was done.

A Zen student showed me to my room. I was excited about sharing a room with a person who was contemplating entering the priesthood. I was intrigued by the idea and I'd be able to watch my roommate up close and see what it's like to aspire to such a life, to take vows. I assumed she knew all about Zen the moment I saw her *hippari,* a Japanese-style work jacket, hanging on the closet door.

Our room was the size of the bedroom I'd shared years earlier with my younger sister. The walls were stark white with two sets of paired windows facing Lily Alley. There were two mantels with drawers, two closets one on each side of the room. I breathed in the smell of sandalwood and sat down on the bed that appeared to be available. The bed across the room was made up with personal blankets. On the mantle on her side of the room was an altar with a picture of San Francisco Zen Center's founder, Suzuki Roshi, a small statue of Buddha, and a mint-green vase of flowers.

I had shared a bedroom with my sister for many years, so I knew how to cope with someone sleeping less than twenty feet away. I knew how to create privacy when there really wasn't any, and create breathing space, recognizing that the bedroom was not my own. However, I was not used to living in a communal building with nearly sixty white-skinned strangers. Had my despair been so great that it had driven me to this? Where was the African spiritual community? Or was this journey of wanting to be sequestered from the world so deep in my bones that it didn't matter with whom?

Perhaps it was from an ancestral place I did not recognize. Didn't ancient Africans meditate before Buddha was even born? Had my ancestors placed me here for my own good?

I affirmed that the gateway of Zen was part of my ancestral and karmic past. It was meant for me to be at Zen Center so I could see how rageful I was at white supremacy and poverty, and how afraid I was of the world. Surprisingly, the teachings came alive rubbing elbows with those who reminded me of the pain in being disrespected. Buddha's teachings came alive through the fear of other people's ignorance.

There was a "them" that was going to hurt me; a "them" not being aware of the suffering "they" caused. By being afraid of "their" unconsciousness, I suffered. If I was afraid, how could I help end suffering in the world? If fear blocked me from touching my own heart, how was I going to live? With fear, how could I hear the cries of the Earth? How could I hear compassion, truth, or injustice that goes beyond my personal wounds? How could I speak truthfully if I can't hear from fear of supremacist or homophobic people? With fear of others causing my suffering, I could not cultivate life, be generous or even aware.

Without addressing this great fear in living, I was not able to take refuge in any wisdom teachings.

When I arrived on the steps of the fifty-year-old institution I reclaimed some of the wisdom I knew from birth. I met an ancient way of being upon the earth before Buddha ever spoke and something from the ever-pervasive source of all our lives. If the light of wisdom was before Buddha, was Zen the right practice for me?

A dream responded to my question. My Zen teacher and another teacher came to me smiling. She said, "We have something for you," and pulled out a small box. In it were what she called Zen shoes. They were tiny. My wide, flat African feet wouldn't possibly be able to fit in them. I gladly received the gift, but in my mind I said, "They're too narrow."

The words "too narrow" suspended themselves in my mind. Was Zen too narrow? Was the spirit world telling me this was not the right home for me? But the spirit world does not choose among practices. There is no Buddhism, Islam, Ifa, Native American tradition, nor Christianity. The dream was pointing to my view of life in general.

My view was too narrow.

At one point much later, after I'd decided to ordain, I called my sisters and told them I was going to Malaysia. Their minds went blank as to where that was. I was headed to the ninth Sakyadhita International Conference on Buddhist Women being held at Sau Seng Lum Temple in Selangor, Puchong. *Sakyadhita* means "the daughter of Buddha."

The traffic was heavy on our way from the Kuala Lumpur Airport to the five-day conference, where I would meet nuns and other women from around the world, women who shared the desire to live a spiritual life, to dedicate their lives to compassion and love. We rode alongside tall and squatting palm trees, lush green bushes, tiny cars, and small SUVs. Inside the cars were Muslim women wrapped in cloth from crown to chin, some from crown to toe.

Our host, who lives in Malaysia, told us that multiple dwellings are built upward to preserve open land. She was shocked when she saw in America one house taking up large plots of land, that one family could have so much to themselves. I knew that's exactly the kind of house I wanted, one with a lot of land, not like the buildings I saw out the window that looked like urban subsidized housing, apartments stacked one upon another.

It became clear that I'd have to let go of many desires I had in becoming a nun. That might have been the moment I gave up relying on my wits to succeed in the material world, trusting that I would be supported spiritually. As one friend put it, "You vowed to poverty." I would say I vowed to simplicity, with or without money.

That afternoon I heard Tibetan nuns singing "We Shall Overcome" from deep in their hearts, affirming they do believe liberation is possible today, not someday. I was on the other side of the curtain that divided a dormitory of lay and ordained women.

I sang "We Shall Overcome" too, a silent rendition.

Tears welled up in my eyes. What brings such a song of freedom to the heart of an African American woman much older than the young Tibetan nuns? Perhaps they longed to be in Tibet. I longed to know what African country my ancestors came from and what language they spoke. Despite our displacement, we women from forty-five countries arrived together at the home of Buddha's daughters. I slept well.

The next morning beneath the granite sky and the prized Malaysian bougainvillea bouncing lightly, the Muslim prayer called out over Puchong, surrounding the temple and my head. Outside in the humid air, barefoot, in my light cotton kimono normally worn under a black Zen practice robe, I hung wet clothes to dry. A smile lit up my face; suddenly I was not from anywhere else in the world than where I stood, feet on the one earth beneath a sliver of a familiar moon not yet set. Longing for ancestry was deferred, in the moment. I was satisfied being in the midst of nuns.

At the opening ceremony, nuns were invited to chant the Heart Sutra from their respective traditions. Kyoshin, an ordained Zen priest from my sangha, and I waited to chant the Heart Sutra in Japanese.

The program coordinator said to us, "Are you Japanese?"

There was a sign on the back of Kyoshin's chair that said "Japanese," designating the row. The row in front of us was designated "Theravada," with nuns from Thailand, Sri Lanka, and Malaysia.

"No," we said, "we're not Japanese. We're American." ·

"Then why are you chanting in Japanese?"

"We were asked to represent Japan for the ceremony?" We cringed, knowing it's not literally possible to represent Japan.

"You speak Japanese?" they asked, looking at my black African face and Kyoshin's European one.

"No, but we chant the Heart Sutra in Japanese at our temple."

"So, you're Japanese?"

"No, we're Americans."

The room was filled with photographers and reporters from Malaysian newspapers and TV, and they photographed the African dressed in a Zen lay robe seated in the section for the Japanese. As they snapped pictures of me I wondered, where are the Japanese anyway?

"There are only two of you?" the coordinators asked.

"Yes."

"Where are the rest of the Japanese?" (This was a good question.)

"Are you nuns?" They glanced at our short-cropped hair standing out among the shaved heads of our Dharma sisters. The sixty or so nuns representing China were chanting. After them, it was time for us to climb the elevated stage and stand in front of a six-foot-high Buddha statue and 300 dignitaries, politicians, and abbots of the largest Buddhist organizations. The conference is important for Malaysian Buddhists, given the country is predominantly Islamic.

A young Malaysian woman tapped me on the shoulder, "Are you from Africa?"

"No."

"Are you Japanese?"

"No, I'm from America and I practice Zen in the Japanese tradition." She smiled, still a bit confused.

When it was our turn to chant, there was only one thing to do: chant the Heart Sutra ("Maka Hannya Haramitta Shin Gyo") as Japanese as possible. I heard our voices echoing out across the silent auditorium as Kyoshin and I stood steadfast, facing the audience. Only two of us on that elevated stage, as if we were standing on a mountain. The sound of our voices seemed to reach the lake a hundred yards away from the open twenty-foot-square temple doorway. I felt a breeze come to the stage, but it turned out to be air from the cooling system. Another breeze I felt my mother standing next to me as a support for doing what seemed to be a strange thing for a black girl from Los Angeles.

After chanting, we bowed to the Buddha, then to the audience, and walked off the stage. Back at my seat, I listened to the Korean nuns whose Heart Sutra sounded most like ours. I felt honored that Kyoshin had invited me to join her. Even though we were in over our heads, we managed to extend our hearts through the chant of compassion.

Later, we were congratulated on how beautifully we chanted and how the voices of the two of us sounded as voluminous as entire groups of nuns. Perhaps it was pure Buddha nature and planting our feet firmly, despite and because of the confusion we brought to the ceremony, that helped our voices project. Perhaps the chant reminded us of being in the Buddha Hall at Zen Center, joined by the sangha back home. Whatever the reason, Kyoshin and I turned to each other and acknowledged that next time we'll bring more women from home.

The next day I spoke at the conference on black people, the history of slavery, and Buddhism. The room went quiet; the cameras stopped flashing. Afterward, there was a genuine interest from the nuns and laywomen from all over the world about the grave situation of African Americans in the U.S., especially black youth. They wanted to know about the possibilities of Buddha's teachings affecting the despair among African Americans. They wanted to know about Buddhism in ancient and contemporary Africa. Presenting the paper turned their focus from struggling to discern my nationality or the origin of my robes to an inquiry into oppression in the light of the Buddha's teachings as a possible refuge for oppressed groups of people. I was unsure, because Buddhism had not yet become a home for me. I was a work in progress at the time.

I walked away from the conference feeling the honor of being referred to as a "venerable." I trusted that being ordained, entering the spiritual path fully could be a way for me to fill the void of lost land, culture, heritage, and belonging. To touch the earth and reach my ancestors through connection with others who believed that was possible, gave me a sense of direction. It didn't matter which tradition of Buddha's teachings or which spiritual path, African, Japanese, or neither.

What was important was that a spiritual path, narrow or wide, might be a portal to freedom. The path would have to be like a pregnant mother, providing the darkness and warmth of a womb, continuous nourishment, and a canal to pass through when I was ready to enter the next phase of life.

Six months prior to ordaining as a priest, I sat in the *zendo* singing Sundance Lakota ceremonial songs in my head. I could hear the one-heart beat of the round drum and see the drum sticks moving in unison. I was sitting for five days at the Tassajara Zen Mountain Center in the Los Padres Forest for *tangaryo*, a ceremony that mimics the monk waiting at the gate to gain entry into Shaolin Monastery, where the teacher was Bodhidharma. That old monk stood outside until the snow came up to his waist and still Bodhidharma did not invite the student in. When the monk cut off his arm showing his sincere desire for the teachings, only then did the teacher let him in. Whether this story is true or apocryphal, Bodhidharma was interested in students willing to let go of what they had embodied in the past in order to make room for the teachings. Will we cut off our limbs to do so? For five days, I sat next to folks I mostly didn't know.

Of course, we could go to the bathroom and drink water. We ate with the other seventy-five residents who were not in tangaryo, and we did go to sleep at 9:00 in the evening only to return to the zendo the next morning at 4:30 to sit again. It took place during horse–fly season. The flies would come into the zendo in the heat of the day, land on my skin, and proceed to bite, a sharp pinching bite. Ignoring any hand waving or movement, they clung tight. Was I supposed to hold still while being attacked? There were also mucus-eating flies that loved the crevices of my ears, the corners of my eyes, and the openings of my nose. I could no longer sit still in the barrage of creatures we were not supposed to swat at or kill.

When the bell rang for a bathroom break, I ran to get toilet tissue. Not to wipe the sweat off my face or beneath the dark robes layered over a kimono and *juban* (a white cotton undershirt), but to stuff in my ears. If I did not hear the buzzing, maybe that would help. I covered exposed skin with insect repellant and returned to the hall ready for the intruders.

It didn't take much to realize what the flies' purpose was. Without them I would have fallen asleep.

When the five days ended, I ran out of the hall and into my room. I had planned to shut the door and keep everyone out. No luck. My dorm-mates came to congratulate me. It was a surprise to be embraced so warmly after suffering so much. Their words were sweet and loving. I decided to stay a while.

During the ninety-day practice periods that were a part of my Zen training, I would swing my legs out of bed every morning at 3:30 so I'd have plenty of time to be in the meditation hall by 4:30. Fortunately, the women's dorm was heated, because it was cold outside. I would look down at my feet and ask, "What are you doing?" The only thing that kept me in this craziness for six months was constant confrontation with myself, and I cried like a child.

In meditation, I was that black girl-child who had suffered in the world. I relived having ponytails and a nicely starched dress. The little girl discovered she was looking for her mother in everyone, no matter what gender, race, or sexual orientation. She was looking for her mother in her lovers, her sisters, her friends, and now in the Zen priests who were mostly white and male. My mother could not be found in these people. This child was desperate for acknowledgment she could never get outside. Where was she a person? Was she loveable?

I did not want to be defeated.

I sat in meditation listening to the noise of past and future mind. It was much louder than I expected. I had reluctantly laid down my armor at the door, as was asked of the thirteenth-century samurai who arrived at the Zen temple to learn to concentrate so they might survive their battles. My motivation was not much different. Would I survive the battles of life having been born in a dark body? What if I was too tired to fight? I wanted to say hush; talking even silently is a distraction. Did I dare look over my shoulder at the spirits of my ancestors waiting to see what would become of their daughter?

At the end of long sits, my mind would be lost and my body aching. I had stared down the enemy inside me, but the battlefield was still full. The massive amount of blood from all the fighting dripped inside where no one could see. I tended leaky old wounds by acknowledging they existed. When the bell rang to end the period of meditation, there was an immense feeling of happiness. I straightened my robe, the shield of protection, and stood upright, in *shashu*, one hand folded over the other against my belly, as if I hadn't struggled for forty minutes. I didn't look anyone in the eye, which is the protocol. I was thankful that no one could see where I'd been.

As others ran to their rooms at the end of the day, I stopped to look up at the galaxy of stars in the dark sky. I could only see the first three or four layers. A Dharma-sister stopped and looked up to see what I might be staring at and then left quickly. I wanted to tell her that I was staring in a mirror and ask whether she could see us. I walked slowly to my room, gliding in black Zen robes, in the midst of ghosts who haunted the sacred land and low-burning lanterns that dotted the path.

The next day, I requested an interview with the teacher leading the practice period. I fumbled trying to sit in a solid mountain position before the teacher, and then I said, "I don't feel loved here." The smell of the straw tatami mats calmed my nerves. I looked at the calligraphy on the wall. The room felt like a cocoon where one gets ready to be transformed.

He said, "Everyone loves you."

I looked at him as though he had lost his mind. His expression remained serious. He was certain of what he had said.

I groaned.

He said, "Yes, everyone loves you, but they don't know it yet."

Another noise came from deep in my throat. Did that mean I loved the strangers at the center but didn't know it yet? It was the most intimate moment between a Zen teacher and myself. I was between an opening and another opening. Time was nonexistent. I glanced toward the door as tears came to my face. In the limitlessness, I had been stripped down to unbearable exposure. It was the same spirit-filled nakedness that I had felt since the first time I stepped into a zendo. At last, intimacy did not require knowing where I came from. It was not even an expression of love. It was the unflinching revelation of myself to myself in the midst of being seen, if only to myself. This intimacy was to be so close to the core of my spirit I could taste it and touch it.

Upon leaving the monastery in the forest and claiming the zendo as home, I entered the path of becoming a Zen priest. My older sister attended the ordination ceremony. To her, Zen Center was a foreign land, but I trusted it wouldn't matter. She loved me and she was going to represent the family no matter how difficult it might be. She too is a warrior.

When I entered the Buddha Hall with the other initiates chanting Shakyamuni Buddha's name, I did not look around. I simply felt the gathering of my people—my drumming and sweat lodge sisters, close friends, dharma brothers and sisters from various places; all were present. Zen teachers were front and center. When they called my new ordination name, *Ekai* (Ocean of Wisdom) *Zenju* (Complete Tenderness) and asked the ancestors to look down upon me, I bowed my newly shaven head in reverence. I gave praise to my mother, my father, and all the ancestors who gave me life.

Zen practice is ancestral work, in an ancestral home.

Upon transmission of light from ancient awakened ones, life becomes an inner bow to the ancestors—offering flowers, ringing bells, and honoring the life we were gifted. We were born with their light; it's in the marrow of our bones. The light of my ancestors became so bright during Dharma transmission, I was able to see my own spirit and become intimate with it. I bowed on my knees, and I was no longer just the creation of my parents but rather the continuation of awakening light from ancestors. Buddha was no longer a person but an expression of light. Freedom had taken up residence. I was a baby, on my knees, facing a new moon. Freedom is the return to this unborn state of mind in which there is wakefulness and reliance on wisdom rather than strategy and armor.

I had not intended for Zen to be the womb that nourished me on the path to a new life. I never sought it out. I wasn't even interested in the teachings. I simply ran into the world to see what would come and take me.

When you don't intend anything, everything happens.

We go along living our lives, there's a rumbling, and the winds blow us somewhere we've never been before. We might be fearful of the new territory of freedom, but in the end, even the delusions that arise in meditation fade, and true meditation surfaces naturally like the scent of jasmine. There is no wanting, hoping, or thinking of life as a grand journey; it's one breath after another. Being a spiritual warrior is not an adventure your friends will praise you for. Sitting for a million hours is not a feat to boast of. It's a treacherous adventure of staying sane, going crazy, and wandering in the stillness naked and hungry until you have found your way home.

In the end, we go absolutely nowhere, and it is exactly where we thought we'd be.

We die unrepaired, unimproved, yet raw and precious.

Earlier, I wrote about yearning for ancestral connection, in particular African ways of being. In this yearning, there is a phenomenal historical "substance," the result of having enslaved ancestors. But I must be careful. When I *long for* an African self, there is a ripening of unwholesome seeds of slavery—being dehumanized and brought to a foreign land. These seeds are part of a collective, stored consciousness of yearning among descendants of the enslaved.

Since ripening takes place every moment, whether we see it or not, by coming to terms with slavery we cease to water the seeds of an atrocity that continues to cause suffering to so many. We can change the seeds of slavery and recover the loss of home. The impact of slavery on people of African descent remains an embodied experience to contend with, but we can simultaneously water the seeds of freedom.

This doesn't mean we forget what happened or even stop speaking of it, but we remove the *longing for what was lost* because of slavery and embrace what is in front of us. Without the longing, slavery, although embodied and remembered, ceases to be an obstruction to finding home. It remains an element of my origin but not the center of my life.

What might happen if those in a sanctuary based on a shared history of atrocity begin to water a seed motivated by freedom and not pain and suffering?

The quality of the sanctuary would become the expression of a renewed consciousness for wellness. We can have a direct experience of our boundlessness, while still understanding the historical origin of our trauma. The sanctuary

of freedom surfaces from an awakened heart that fully recognizes an historical experience *and* the absolute availability
of peace. With freedom, we begin to participate in our destiny and not fear or live in reaction to the wrath of oppres-
sors or dominant cultures. We bloom rather than whither
away in our suffering. Thich Nhat Hanh calls cultivating
wholesome seeds, "transformation at the base."

When we establish sanctuary from a place of mat-
uration, the gateway opens wide. We are tied not only to
the elements of fire, water, earth, and air, but are free in
space, time, and place. This transformation is dependent
on understanding we have a karmic conditioning, which is
temporal and constructed through our life experiences, but
we are also free from such conditioning. The path of finding
home in the context of freedom is to see and engage *both*
as interdependent. A sanctuary, within or without, built on
such freedom is one in which complete refuge is possible
and true home can come into being.

In a lucid dream after an emotionally painful time, a
healer came to me and said, "Here is a tool to dig with.
When you see yourself, add nothing from the past." The
self is not in the past, present, or the future but is in a time
of being or *uji* as Dogen called it. Time is being. If we are
not in time being, we will yearn for the past or future and
manipulate the present. Time is existence, and existence is
time. If we *are*, time is. When we understand that we are *in
time* together, everywhere, we can see and create sanctuary
in the ordinariness of everyday life. We can see a blade of
grass or marker in a patch of mud as sanctuary.

Being ordinary, or oppressed, is not a limitation to creating a life that has meaning, a life that is rewarding, if we

understand how we have been conditioned. Zen teacher Dainin Katagiri said, "Living in the world, seeing the total picture of beings interchanging one with the other, if I say 'I,' simultaneously the other's life is there." He is speaking of a collective "I" like the collective you in "you all."

The content of our lives is not just *our* lives. Our ordinariness and oppression is collective.

Our home country today faces a resurgence of hatred by those who fear the destruction of their sense of supremacy. They cannot face the final chapter of their centuries-old way of living, and to them it feels like the end of life as they know it. We hear their rants as our nation experiences an increase in hate crimes with no credible response from those in power. Millions of Americans, mostly black and brown people, face discrimination, religious persecution, the destruction of families through deportation, and even the possibility of internment as was done to Americans of Japanese ancestry during World War II. Even though racism is in America's DNA, we hadn't expected to see such blatant dehumanization and annihilation in the 21st century.

When what has gone unacknowledged surfaces, it feels like a new reality, but we know in our hearts it is not new. There can be no better answer to our meditations and prayers for dissolving hatred than for it to be placed front and center and exposed. What is our truth? Have our actions been ineffective? Have we relied *only* on prayer and meditation or *only* on social activism? When a shift in a system takes place, especially one that causes fear and discomfort, it allows for something strikingly different to appear, furthering our growth as individuals and as a community of people.

Many of us have been practicing Buddha's teachings or walking other spiritual paths for what feels like forever, preparing for major challenges. We've been waiting for this time to create a home that mirrors the compassion and freedom in our hearts. We are ready. Our rage, pain, and anger need to be exposed so we can transform and mature with them.

Now is the time we have been practicing for.

Acknowledgments

To those who have held me, fed me, and housed me, I express great gratitude. Thank you to Andy Francis, Josh Bartok, and Arnie Kotler for editing and trusting my words. I give thanks to all communities and sanctuaries that invited me in and helped to grow the Earth that I am. I bow to my family and beloved who constantly support my creativity and trust my integrity. I send the merit of this work out to those who involuntarily live on the streets. May they find shelter in whatever form it takes. May they be well all the days of their lives.

About the Author

Rev. Zenju Earthlyn Manuel, PhD, a Soto Zen priest, was born to parents who migrated from rural Louisiana and settled in Los Angeles, where she was born and raised with her two sisters. She is the author of *The Way of Tenderness: Awakening Through Race, Sexuality, and Gender*, with a foreword by novelist Charles Johnson (Wisdom Publications), and *Tell Me Something About Buddhism*, with a foreword by Thich Nhat Hanh (Hampton Roads Publishing). She is the compiler and editor of the award-winning *Seeds for a Boundless Life: Zen Teachings from the Heart* (Shambhala Publications) by Zenkei Blanche Hartman. She is contributing author to many other books including *Dharma, Color, and Culture: New Voices in Western Buddhism* (Parallax), *Hidden Lamp: Stories from Twenty-Five Centuries of Awakened Women* (Wisdom Publications), and author and illustrator of the popular *Black Angel Cards: 36 Oracle Cards and Messages for Divining Your Life* (Kasai River). For more information go to zenju.org.

What to Read Next
from Wisdom Publications

THE WAY OF TENDERNESS
Awakening through Race, Sexuality, and Gender
Zenju Earthlyn Manuel
Foreword by Dr. Charles Johnson

"Manuel's teaching is a thought-provoking, much-needed addition to contemporary Buddhist literature."—*Publishers Weekly*

DREAMING ME
Black, Baptist, and Buddhist: One Woman's Spiritual Journey
Jan Willis

One of *Time Magazine*'s Top Religious Innovators for the New Millennium.

AWAKENING TOGETHER
The Spiritual Practice of Inclusivity and Community
Larry Yang
Forewords by Jan Willis, Sylvia Boorstein

"I don't see how *Awakening Together: The Spiritual Practice of Inclusivity and Community* could be better. It is so wise, thoughtful, and dedicated to our healthful growth, ease, and enlightenment through the Dharma, that I know I will be reading it for years to come. Larry Yang seems to have thought of everything we will need as we venture bravely forward—through racism, prejudice, ignorance, and poor home training—into the free spiritual beings we were meant to be. Together."—Alice Walker, author of *The Color Purple*

About Wisdom Publications

Wisdom Publications is the leading publisher of classic and contemporary Buddhist books and practical works on mindfulness. To learn more about us or to explore our other books, please visit our website at wisdompubs.org or contact us at the address below.

Wisdom Publications
199 Elm Street
Somerville, MA 02144 USA

We are a 501(c)(3) organization, and donations in support of our mission are tax deductible.

Wisdom Publications is affiliated with the Foundation for the Preservation of the Mahayana Tradition (FPMT).